Kiss & Tell:

A Guide to writing Toe-Curling swoon

Kiss & Tell:

A Guide to writing Toe-Curling Swoon

Quill & Flame
PUBLISHING HOUSE

AJ Skelly

Quill & Flame
PUBLISHING HOUSE

Kiss and Tell: A Guide to Writing Toe-Curling Swoon

Romance

A love story.

Kiss and Tell

We humans crave connection. We crave closeness. We crave to be fully known, loved, valued, and desired for who we are. The good, the bad, and the awkward. Most humans, above all, desire that intimate sort of connection shown in romance. It's an integral part of the general human makeup.

What is romance, anyway?

Romance is largely defined as *a love story*.

The first several definitions of the word *romance* in the dictionary all deal with stories—with chivalry, with love, with wooing, with the connecting of two hearts. True romance *does* seek to know, to love despite flaws and faults. Finding that all-encompassing romance can be a challenge—which is one reason people have for hundreds of years been writing stories about discovering the perfect significant other. It's certainly enjoyable to read, as is evidenced by the *millions* of romance books that are consumed each year, but for writers, getting it just right can be difficult...and it can be awkward!

It can be difficult to take such a private moment and turn it into something for public viewing on the page while still keeping the intimacy of the moment. How do you write believable romance that transcends the page? How do you write a kiss on the page that's less awkward than a first kiss between teenagers with braces that get locked together?

Writing about such intimate, potentially awkward, vulnerable moments can be an enormous challenge. There's more to romance than the mashing together of lips, more than the mingling of body parts, more than lust, and more than *only* emotions.

Much like when hot water and ice are combined, they create steam—when vulnerability that encompasses the emotional *and* physical elements combines well on the page, authors create *swoon*.

And *swoon* is the thing that sets good romantic writing apart from the rest.

So, let's talk about how to write swoon.

Swoon

The act of making a reader fall in love with your characters, feel all the feels, and be utterly hungover upon the finishing of your book.

WHAT IS SWOON?

*S*woon is the driving force behind the romance that fills your chest and makes you feel right along with the characters in the moment. It's a buildup. It's slow. It's not immediate (or if it is immediate, there are consequences that take half the book to undo and right the impetuousness). It's the tension, the angst, the emotional tethers between characters that keep the reader reading, anticipating, rooting for, dying for that moment of emotional release between characters when they finally come together—either in an emotional sense, or in the locking of lips, or even behind a closed door.

At its heart, romance is meant to be personal and intimate, and that raises many questions surrounding the writing of good romance. How much is too much? When should my characters kiss? Do I want them to kiss at all? What can a kiss convey that words cannot? What other actions should show this blooming romance? Must my characters have a physical relationship to have romance?

Writing swoon means creating an emotional pull between the reader and the characters. Without this emotional pull, the kiss won't produce the satisfaction the reader desires. The swoonless story might still be compelling and enjoyable, but the most satisfying kisses end with the reader's emotional investment being wholly sat-isfied.

In this writing guide, you'll find ways to incorporate swoon into your writing at several different heat levels. For the purposes of this guide, we'll define our romance levels to Sweet, Swoony, and Steamy. Swoon, in all its forms, is different from erotica or smut, and it's different from writing all the details on the page. *Swoon* implies *romance*, not necessarily the physical act of sex. While the two can be conjoined (no pun intended), there are often very different readers for each genre.

This guide will provide you with the tools you need to write romance that is swoony at several different heat levels (Sweet, Swoony, and Steamy), but will not cross into open door territory.

In addition to exploring ways to craft romantic heat levels and kisses, this guide will walk you through each of the five things needed to create SWOON:

    1. Attraction

    2. Emotion

    3. Reaction

    4. Vulnerability

    5. Physical Action

What are some of the swooniest books or TV/movies you've read or watched? What made them feel so swoony to you?

Let us think of swoon...

What are some of the swooniest books or TV/Movies you've enjoyed?

____
____
____
____
____

What are some instances in books or TV/Movies where you felt uncomfortable with the romance?

____
____
____
____
____

Why did you enjoy them?

____
____
____
____

Why did it make you uncomfortable?

____
____
____
____

To Create Swoon

1) Attraction

2) Emotion

3) Reaction

4) Vulnerability

5) Physical Action

ROMANCE
IS A
JOURNEY

Romance is a Journey

As all good stories are, romance, too, is a journey. Getting characters from point A to point B where the reader swoons alongside them is not a quick trip to the mini mart. It's a journey. One that takes deliberation, consideration, and declaration.

There are a few key aspects that should be addressed to embark on this journey of swoony romance: Characters, Setting, Progression, and Believability.

The first key aspect we will encounter are the characters.

Characters

When you write *swoon*, the characters drive the emotion, and they drive the plot. It's harder to have swoon in a plot-focused book. When swoon is the goal, it is the characters who must be the centrifugal force in the story.

Plot is necessary. One cannot have a story without plot, but when swoon is the end goal, it will be the characters who inform the plot, not vice versa.

Now.

Who are your characters?

Flip over the next two pages and look at the provided "characters." Fill in the blanks to flesh these people out inside your head. Give them names, because we'll come back to them.

How would these two characters interact with each other?

Would they be like oil and water? Or would they mesh immediately?

Write a few paragraphs on the next pages that show how these two characters might meet for the first time.

Man's Name	♡	Woman's Name

Man's Name

Where is he from?

What is his family background?

What time period is he from?

Likes and dislikes

What culture is he from?

Hobbies?

Hair color?

Eye color?

Woman's Name

Hobbies?

Hair color?

Eye color?

Likes and dislikes

Where is she from?

What is her family background?

What time period is she from?

What culture is she from?

Man	Woman

♡

Quirks?	Quirks?
__________	__________
__________	__________
__________	__________
__________	__________
__________	__________

Wounds	Wounds
__________	__________
__________	__________
__________	__________
__________	__________
__________	__________

Anything else about them:	Anything else about them:
__________	__________
__________	__________
__________	__________
__________	__________
__________	__________
__________	__________

Setting

Now that we have the characters established, let us look at the second part of this romantic journey. The setting.

Setting is the time and place in which your story takes place. If you think about it, the setting is a hugely important part of how the story takes shape. Many sensory details you might include in your story are dependent upon the setting.

The geographical setting of a story is like a framework for how the story unfolds. The story must conform to the confines of geography. Mountains. Lake. Ocean. Underwater. Modern world. Ancient civilization. Frontier. Medieval castle. Boston. On a pirate ship.

In addition to geography, the time period makes an enormous difference. If the story is set in modern times at a corporate mountain retreat, that's a lot different than if the story takes place in the same mountains four centuries earlier when the Fae roamed the woods and bears stopped and sat down for a chat. The time period directly affects how characters navigate their terrain. Do they have cell phones? Do they have a telegraph? Are they relegated to smoke signals across a wide expanse? Do they use magic?

A note on worldbuilding here.

When writing fantasy, often magic is employed. This becomes part of the landscape of the story. But, hear this, use your magic responsibly.

Every world that has magic must have rules. Rules form the basis for your world. As the author, you are able to bend or change those rules as you need to in order to fit the confines of your story, but make sure that your rules and your magic system make sense, and make sure your characters fit within those rules and that system. If they don't, tying your swoon into your magical world will be difficult and may feel disingenuous to your readers.

Think about the characters you just created. Think about them in a few different time periods, and think about how that might affect how they were perceived and how they would have to change or how it might impact them in other ways. Does your character love milk chocolate? Milk chocolate wasn't invented until the late 1600s, and even then, more time passed before it became the tasty candy bars of today. Small details make or break a story, and the setting determines a surprising lot of those small details. Those small details that often come from the setting can be used to enhance your romance.

As you are crafting your story, think about how the place and the time will impact not only the overall journey of the story, but also the characters themselves. Remember, in a swoony story, it's the characters who do the bulk of the work. But even so, the setting will inform how those characters thrive, suffer, respond, and ultimately grow.

Read this excerpt from OF FLAME & FROST. To set the stage, the two main characters, Aspen and Cole, have ice and fire powers, respectively. They are trapped in the past at a magical academy, trying to find a specific type of magic that will take them back to their time.

Both have some painful elements in their past, and they've been fighting their attraction for nearly thirty chapters at this point in the story.

All of this aside, look at how the fantasy, the magic, and the setting—the magic of the world—itself play into this swoony scene.

We snuck to the library without a chance meeting with any Brownies or the ogre.

Must, dust, and the ancient smell of parchment met us as we moved into the enormous room.

Aspen yawned, triggering one of my own.

"I'm seriously contemplating a nap," she said, glancing about the dark room.

"Let me warn you that the floor is hard. But I could go for a nap myself."

Eventually we settled together near the granite stair-case and finished our food. Aspen had packed more in her pocket, which I appreciated. I was still hungry and concerned about my fuel reserves. But once I'd eaten more, I felt full and sleepy. I propped my back up against the stone, leery of falling too deeply asleep in an unprotected area. Aspen rested her head on my shoulder, her shiny hair falling over me like cornsilk.

Moments later, her even breathing told me she was asleep. My eyelids drooped, my heart content for the moment with Aspen next to me. It was strange to be so content while still aware of the impending danger surrounding the Academy and possibly impacting whether or not we'd ever see our own home again. My eyes closed.

Sometime later I woke with a crick in my neck, which I quickly forgot about as I realized Aspen was still sleeping against me, one of her arms casually thrown across my waist, her head on my chest.

My heart thumped. She trusted me. Completely. In spite of the damage I caused wherever I went.

Syrai's ruined face flashed across my memories, her screams of terror and pain clashing in my ears, causing me to wince.

"Cole?" Aspen sat up sleepily, her hand finding my chest right over my drumming heart.

"I'm here." The words were strangled and tight in my throat.

"What's wrong?"

I sighed. How did I tell her I had fallen for her? How could I tell her that after what happened with Syrai? That I wanted her but could never have her? The possibility of hurting her was too great. Even if she was the Ice Queen, I was still afraid the monster inside me might rear its head again and melt her completely. Even if the monster had been strangely subdued of late.

My hand trailed down her hair.

"Do you suppose Alger-Aodh will be dropping by anytime soon?" I asked instead. I didn't want to move, but some distance between us would help me clear my head. My insides were burning up with her pressed against me.

"I have no idea what time it is."

"Me neither. My back needs to pop," I said, needing space before I did something stupid.

"I could stretch, too."

I stood stiffly and reached a hand down to pull her to her feet.

Her hand was cool and delicate in my hot grasp. As she straightened, her chest brushed mine and without knowing how it happened, my hands were suddenly on her waist.

Electricity charged the air between us.

I felt the sparks floating in my eyes and the burning she caused inside me threatened to explode. Different from my usual fire, but with no less potential for destruction. Hers.

Aspen's hand snaked out and cupped my jaw.

Her breath was cool on my face. My knees went weak.

"Aspen." Her name was a plea on my lips.

Hers were pink and parted, inches from mine. My fingers tightened around her waist, sitting directly above the curve of her hips. Blood and fire crashed through me, threatening to burst me wide open.

"Cole, do you want to kiss me?"

"You know I do." The words rasped themselves from my throat. My pulse pounded, and her skin was frigid beneath her shirt and my burning hands.

"Your fire won't hurt me. It can't hurt me." Her whisper of cool breath hit my face, and my resolve crumbled. Her lips were an inch away from mine. Longing made my flaming limbs tremble. Her chest was pressed against mine, and I couldn't tell if the frantic beating was my heart or hers.

Her hand slid up my neck and into the hair at the base of my neck.

I think I groaned.

Quick as lightning, she grazed her lips across mine. I jerked back, terrified wanting searing through me. The taste of her melted on my lips.

Her fingers rested against the pulse pounding in my neck. She bore no blisters. No marks of my heat. She was not Syrai. She was frost. She was snow. She was ice.

She was waiting. Her blue eyes were clear. With a shiver of pleasure, I realized she wanted me to kiss her as much as I wanted to.

Something broke within me and for the first time in four years, I let go of my fear. Fear of what I could do. I gripped ahold of my internal flames, vowing that I wouldn't let them hurt Aspen.

Aspen who saw me. Saw my ugliness, saw the monster inside, knew what it had done, and wanted me still. Within her gaze, I found the part of me that was who I used to be. The Cole I was before the accident. The flicker of life inside me that I liked about myself. It was okay to be who I was, half of one thing and not quite all of another. The two halves of me, both phoenix and fire-drake, made me who I was. I chose to be worthy of the trust she placed in me. Fledgling confidence settled in the flames racing through my core as my fear floated up, taking its choking hold with it.

So slowly I thought I might break from the wanting of it, I lowered my lips to hers. White hot fire danced across my lips, down my arms, blazed in my fingertips as I gripped her close.

I'd thought about it, dreamed about it, wanted it, but never thought it was within my grasp. Until now. Her lips burned in a way that I wanted to consume me. We bumped awkwardly together as we tried to find the way our lips best fit together. My knees went weak, and I wasn't sure live flames weren't bursting through my skin. Her mouth was cold against mine, fire and ice together and sending my head spinning. My hands wrapped around her middle, holding her close. Her fingers traced my jaw in a tingling trail of cold that sent a fresh wave of heat roiling through me.

And she was right. The hotter I burned, the colder she froze until a great cloud of steam enveloped us.

Our lips tangled together, frigid bursts against the lava inside me. A flash of heat surrounded by freeze. It was intoxicating. Aspen was intoxicating. My hands slid from her back to her sides. She reached up on tiptoe, her lips pressing harder against mine, and I was sure I'd combust.

We finally broke apart, steam pouring off us in all the places we touched. Flame and frost swirled together in a cloud of hazy, vaporous longing. For a long moment, we just stood there, searching the other's face, breathing harder than normal. Savoring what we'd just created together between the two of us. Aspen grasped the back of my head as she leaned her forehead against my shoulder.

My hand slid down her silky hair, and I leaned my ear against her head. My heart thrummed. Closing my eyes, I tried to memorize every thought and feeling pinwheeling through me.

"Cole!"

The urgency in her voice shook me from my memorization.

Suddenly fearful that I was hurting her, some latent reaction to my fire despite everything, I leaped back, knocking my head into the underside of the staircase.

She gripped my hand, and I breathed a sigh of relief as she looked at me, high color in her cheeks, but from the fire I'd kindled in her, not the fire of my skin.

Gingerly she reached out and grasped a tiny strand of magenta magic off my shoulder.

"Cole," she whispered. My mouth gaped.

"Where did that come from?" My voice was still rough, still completely affected by our kiss.

Aspen's eyebrows drew together. She looked around, and as she moved, I noticed the magenta dusting on her cheek like bright pink icing sugar.

"Aspen, you've got some more of the dust on your face." She stilled and let me brush my thumb over it. The steam still hanging around was damp enough that my thumb turned the dust into a smudge on her cheek.

"Oh, it prickles. Is it like the dust we found up in the tower?"

"Yeah." A thought was niggling at the back of my brain, trying to push itself through the haze of wonder that still drummed through me.

"Hold onto that string," Aspen said.

I had two seconds to tighten my grip on the filmy strand of magic before Aspen's lips were back on mine.

We kissed. I was pretty sure it was the best thing that had ever happened to me.

"Was there an ulterior motive for that?" I asked her, still a little breathless as she pulled back.

"Look at the magic." Her chest was still going up and down faster than normal, her eyes wide and animated as she tipped back far enough to look at me, her hand still braced against my bicep.

I glanced at the magic. My eyes bulged. It had grown.

It was easily twice the size it had been, its filmy gossamer surface sparkling like it was a newly minted coin, pulsing with its potential power.

"We made this." I heard the amazement in my own voice.

"We can go home." Aspen's words were hushed with wonder.

Our eyes met, unspoken excitement, fear, and trepidation flowing between us. But how could we leave now? Now that the Academy was at stake? Could we help win the battle we both knew was coming?

"We can't leave now," Aspen whispered.

"I know."

It is the setting—both the place and the magic built into the fabric of the story—in this scene that lends itself to the swoon. The magic becomes part of the catalyst of their kiss. Their internal powers inform how they approach it. Cole is afraid; Aspen is fearless. One is hesitant, the other confident, but together, with the magic of the world, it combines to enhance the swoon factor. The combination of the characters, their magic, and the overall setting are integral to the build-up to their swoon. If there was no magic in this scene, it would just be kissing. But because there is a fantastical element, the kiss produces literal magic.

Go to the next page and jot some notes about how the setting of your story might impact the two characters you just created.

Setting

How do your characters change if the story takes place in:

Medieval England

Underwater Kingdom

Fantasy World

Outer Space Exploration Vessel

1776

A Holiday Party

Small Town

Antarctica

Progression

PROGRESSION

The next part of the romantic journey is progression.

Swoon needs build-up. Just like any story would develop, the romance must also percolate, mature, and reach its full potential for the biggest impact on your reader. For the maximum potency, readers first need to know your characters, feel what they feel, want what they want; then readers will lose their literary minds when the characters finally have their swoony moment. While it's possible to have swoon in a piece of flash fiction, the most rewarding swoon in book form will come about three-fourths of the way through the book.

When romance is a driving plot, or a strong subplot, it should follow the regular progression of a story. Freytag's Pyramid is a standard representation of the stages of a story. Look at Freytag's Pyramid on the next page.

Freytag's Pyramid

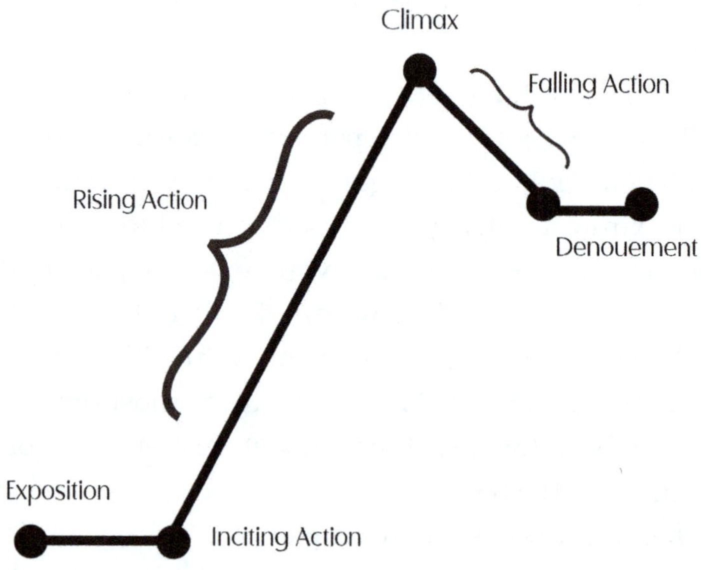

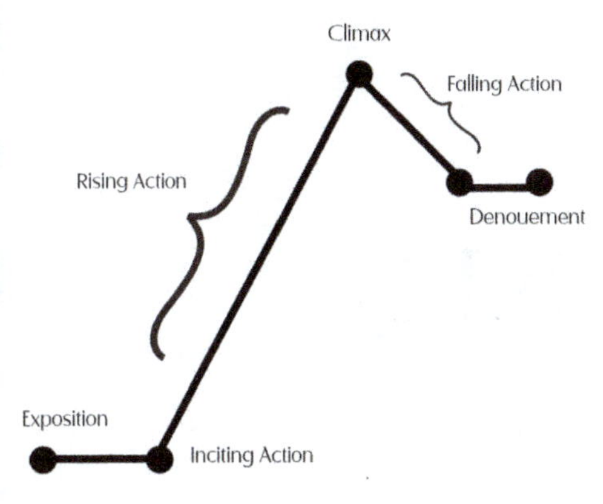

Exposition: Introduce the characters and the setting (time and place)

Inciting Action: Introduce the "big problem" that must be resolved by the end of the story

Rising Action: This is where the bulk of the story takes place, where the tension builds, builds, and builds such that it's ready to explode

Climax: The part where the building tension DOES explode; this is the turning point of the story

Falling Action: The climax is resolved, and loose ends are tied up. The characters' problems are resolved (in whatever manner the story calls for). The characters overcome the big challenge set out in the Inciting Action

Denouement: The end

The culmination of the swoon in your story should culminate in this same general pattern, whether it is the main plot or a sub plot.

Believability

The last part we'll discuss in the romantic journey is believability.

You've created your characters. You've created the world. You know the time period and the setting. But now you must chart the course of progression.

And it must be *believable*.

When your characters set off on their epic journey to swoondom, their actions need to be in keeping with who they are, with their character as you've developed it. Their actions are not just devices to move the plot.

Remember, when swoon is the goal, it's the characters who move the plot, not the plot moving the characters. Ideally, they'll move in tandem, but deference should be given to the characters.

Think of each character as a completed person. Some authors even give their characters personality tests to figure out the ins and outs of their minds. What makes them vulnerable? What makes them tick? What flaws do they have? How are those things going to affect their actions within the story? How will that make them react in certain situations?

When making characters believable, giving them flaws is a great way to make them realistic. Note, flaws are deep, emotive things, not just a physical limitation like walking with a limp. While it's fine to have those, a character who has been deeply wounded in the past and therefore has a hard time trusting anyone is more interesting than a character who is perfectly normal but needs glasses.

Conflicting goals are also a great way to add depth and relatability to your characters. Conflicting goals are when a character wants two things but must sacrifice one to achieve the other. These can get particularly challenging when the heart is involved.

Go to the next page and jot down some ideas for character flaws that might make your characters A and B more believable. Then brainstorm ways those flaws might impact their romantic journey.

Flaws   Flaws

How might these flaws influence their romantic journey?

Swoon is a Thermostat

There are different types, or levels, of swoon and different ways to achieve each.

Keep in mind that the *type* of book you are writing will determine the level of your swoon. Who is your reading audience? What are their expectations for your genre? Different genres have different expectations. The expectation for a sweet, clean regency romance will have wildly different expectations than a regency bodice ripper. Flashing one's ankles in 1800s England is quite different from flashing one's ankles in a 1990s night club. These are things to think about as you're crafting swoon into your plot.

For our purposes, we will use and discuss three main classifications of swoon.

Sweet

Swoony

Steamy

What do you think each level means? Jot your notes on the next page.

Jot down some
words that come
to mind when
you think Sweet,
Swoony, and
Steamy.

Sweet

Sweet Romance focuses more on feelings, emotions, and connection than any kind of physical acts. The emphasis is on emotional intimacy, and may include chaste kissing.

Sweet

Sweet romance focuses more on feelings, emotions, and connection than any kind of physical acts. The emphasis is on emotional intimacy. There are not a lot of descriptors of any sort of physical attribute unless it is the eyes, or perhaps facial features and expressions.

With sweet swoon, typically the culmination of the climax involves a gentle, emotional high. There may be holding of hands; brushing of arms; deep, emotional stares; and searching of faces. Characters often share a brief, chaste kiss—not long or drawn out. Sweet kisses fall into the lightest romance category of stories.

Sometimes, sweet romance doesn't have kissing at all. Sometimes there's just an emotional climax in which two characters recognize their affection or come to an emotional realization.

Read the *sweet* excerpt below that contains emotional recognition with no kissing.

The Winter Gala.

The one function I'd been dreaming of for weeks. Tonight was the night Tyler Crawson would notice me.

I'd had a crush on him for ages but lacked the courage to do anything about it. I'd let my first two years of university slide by without letting him know of my interest. Not tonight. With bravery I didn't feel, I stepped boldly into the dance hall.

Music pealed and lights twinkled. Bright strands of colored lights floated effortlessly through the air, reflecting off the old stone walls of the ancient building now festooned with tinsel and evergreen.

With my best friend Aida next to me and her earlier pep talk still ringing in my ears, I gulped, trying to calm my frantic heartbeat.

"You've got this, girl." Aida winked at me. The flashing red and green lights bounced off her caramel-colored skin. Her ebony hair, curled tight as springs, absorbed the lights and shadows alike. I wished it would absorb my anxiety.

"Breathe, Lainey." She looked me over once more and nodded in satisfaction. "That red sequin dress is perfect. You sparkle like fairy dust." Her plump lips pursed, and she reached behind my ear and smoothed a strand of my white-blonde hair, piled on top of my head. Patting the piece into place, she smiled. "There. Now you're radiant."

A bronze head bobbed on the other side of the room. My heart seized.

Target acquired.

My knees knocked and sweat ghosted my palms.

"I'm going to go have a cup of punch." Aida was on the social committee, and having a cup of punch was her excuse to check on things, but also to leave me to The Plan.

The Plan to approach Tyler. With a final squeeze on my shoulder, she was off, and I was left staring at Tyler's head as it dipped and weaved throughout the crowd.

The music was loud. Too loud. It vibrated up my legs.

I swept up a handful of my shimmery skirt so my feet wouldn't tangle in the hem. I straightened my back and gathered my determination.

I'd only gone a few bodies deep into the crowd when a hand reached out and snatched mine.

"Keiran!" I gasped. Keiran had been one of my closest friends since middle school.

"Lainey. Wow. You look…" he trailed off as his eyebrows rose to his black hairline. He was all dark where I was pale. The tips of his ears colored slightly, but I couldn't tell if that was just from the red lights.

Searching the crowd again, I found Tyler's head. He was only a few yards to my right.

"Looking for Tyler?" Keiran broke in dryly.

"Yes. Tonight he's finally going to see me as more than the smart girl in astrophysics class." I practically hissed the words between my teeth.

Keiran's expression soured. "You don't want him, Lainey. You really don't."

Anger and the sting of unintended betrayal crept into my belly. I glared at Keiran. Wasn't he supposed to be on my side?

"Lainey Rowan? Wow, looking hot, babe!"

The voice froze my blood, and Keiran could probably see the whites of my eyes.

Plastering a smile on my face that I hoped didn't look too deranged, I turned.

"Hey, Tyler." My voice came out higher than it should have. Maybe he didn't notice over the boom of the music.

Without any preamble, Tyler grabbed my hand and put his other low on my waist and swung me onto the dance floor. Keiran grunted somewhere behind me.

We danced for long glorious moments. I was in ecstasy. The song wasn't particularly slow, but it wasn't fast. We moved together, faster than a slow dance, but no weird gyrating. Which was fine, because it let me savor every second of Tyler's hands on my waist without worrying if I was writhing appropriately to the music.

When the song ended, Tyler's copper-colored eyes gazed into mine. My hand fisted into his lapel without my permission. A smile crooked his lips as his eyes roved over my face and one eyebrow rose.

Slowly he leaned down and let his lips caress my cheek. Figurative fireworks blasted out my ears.

"Don't go anywhere," he whispered huskily against my ear. "I'll be back in a few." His big hand squeezed my side before his fingers slowly trailed away.

I'm pretty sure I grew roots right there on the parquet floor.

I don't know how long I stood there like an idiot in the middle of the room, but I came to when Keiran tugged on my hand.

"Keiran, did you see?" I sighed. "He's glorious."

Keiran snorted, his standard pessimism showing. His forehead furrowed, his heavy black brows hanging low over his eyes as his mouth tugged into a thin line.

"You need to see something," he muttered as he grabbed my hand and pulled me through the throng of students and out the arched doorway into the quiet corridor.

Keiran stopped us beside one of the heavy tapestries that lined the antechambers outside the great hall.

"Look. I..." He trailed off and ran a hand through his black hair. "I don't want to show you this, but consider the truth my gift to you this year."

My eyebrows drew together again as he pulled me down the passageway. We crept to the end where it was deserted. His gaze met mine as he put a long finger against his lips, then motioned with his head for me to look around the corner.

Unsure, I peeked out just enough to get an eyeful.

My hand flew to my silent mouth.

There was the boy who'd kissed my cheek moments before. Who had looked at me like I was the center of the world. The boy on whom I'd hung my hopes for years.

He was necking a gorgeous red-head. And his hands...were not appropriately placed. My eyes burned as I turned and fled soundlessly back down the corridor.

I sagged onto a stone bench in a deserted hallway—far away from the snogging couple—who for all I knew were no longer snogging and had moved on to other things. I swiped angrily under one eye. Keiran slowly sat beside me. He ran his hands over the tops of his legs and gusted a sigh.

"I'm sorry, Lainey. I know you liked him. He doesn't *see* you. Doesn't know how special you are." He hesitated and swallowed hard. "Maybe you should look at someone who has seen you all along."

The sincerity in his tone jerked my gaze to his. His chocolate eyes swam with hesitant vulnerability, and my heart lurched painfully in my chest. Sudden realization bloomed in my chest as he sat there, risking his heart, letting me see plainly what he'd kept hidden inside.

He *did* see me.

Keiran had *always* seen me. He'd seen me when I was all awkward limbs and angles. When I won the science award in eighth grade. When I burned my bangs off with a malfunctioning curling iron. When I dropped strawberry frosting all down my shirt. When my gran passed away. When I'd graduated high school with honors. He'd been right beside me. He'd seen *me.*

A heaviness around my heart lifted as I stared at his face, my eyes tracing every line of his messy hair, his reddened ears, his strong jaw, his dark eyes fringed in thick lashes, the tilt of his lips. The intensity and vulnerability in his eyes.

"I see you, Lainey," he whispered roughly.

And for the first time, I saw him, too.

Even though the main characters don't kiss, the emotional connection here is strong. There is vulnerability, there is restraint, there is a confession. The emotions make the climax, rather than any physical action. There is some very light physical touching—when Keiran grabs Lainey's hand—and it's juxtaposed against the physical attraction shown by Tyler. Tyler puts his hands on Lainey's waist. He kisses her cheek. The physical pull is evidenced there, but the emotional pull is shown between Keiran and Lainey. The two act as foils for each other.

Sweet romance can also include light kissing. Let us pick up Keiran and Lainey's story some weeks later.

Keiran's confession had shifted my world on its axis. It had been four weeks, nearly to the day, since the Winter Gala. Since my years-long pining for Tyler Crawson had come to an abrupt end. Since Keiran had bared his soul to me. Since I'd stopped to reevaluate my romantic ideals.

And I was surprised at how much thoughts of Keiran had invaded my daily life. He'd remained the same friend he'd always been, but there was a new awareness of him that sparked across my skin and brought a flush to my cheeks whenever he was in the vicinity. He seemed to be completely unaffected, which was both perplexing and infuriating. I didn't know what he was thinking, I didn't know what he wanted, and I wasn't sure what I wanted either, but I was beginning to have a sneaking suspicion that what I wanted with Keiran wasn't just friendship.

In fact, I wasn't even suspicious.

I was quite certain.

I wanted something *more* with Keiran.

"Can you pass me that sparkly hair pin?" Aida asked as she stood in front of the mirror of our shared dorm room.

"Sure. Gold or silver?"

"Gold."

I passed the hairpin, and she deftly anchored a tiny braid with it. I sighed, staring at my own reflection. Same wide gray eyes, white-blonde hair, and tiny smattering of freckles.

"What's with the long face? You've been mopey all day. You should be excited. We've got a Christmas party to go to!" Aida speared me with a glance. "You're not still thinking about Tyler Crawson, are you?" Her brows drew together in concern. She was well aware that I'd carried a torch for my high school crush for years, and she was also well aware of why and when I'd decided he was not dating material.

I shook my head. "No. I haven't thought about him—well, thought about him in that way—since the Winter Gala." I sighed.

Aida stopped fiddling with the ends of her hair, stilling to give me her full attention. "That sounded like an I'm-thinking-of-a-boy sigh."

I smiled bitterly. "Maybe it was. I don't know."

"Spill it, girl." She swiveled on her chair, dark eyes lighting, slavering for details.

I chuckled. "It's all a mess. I didn't say anything at the time because my brain was too full of stupid Tyler Crawson and because I didn't know what I should do about it, or if I should do anything about it." I paused. Aida leaned forward in her chair, hands clasped in front of her. "You know Keiran was the one who showed me what Tyler was really like...but that night, Keiran also insinuated that maybe *he* liked *me*."

Aida squealed so loud that I winced as she threw up her hands and clapped. "Yes! Finally!" She pumped her fist in the air.

I blinked, mouth falling open. "*Finally?* What does that mean?"

"Oh, Lainey. I've suspected Keiran has liked you for a *long* time. I didn't know if he'd ever do anything about it though. You never saw anyone besides Tyler Crawfish-face. So, are you guys..." She trailed off, eyes expectant.

I groaned and covered my face with my hands. "I don't know," I mumbled into my fingers. I jerked my head back up. "We've been friends for years. He tells me this, then doesn't act any differently. Never says another word, *nothing*! I have no idea what to think."

Aida tipped back in her chair, tapping her lower lip with a glittery red fingernail. "Do you like him back?"

Nothing like getting straight to the point.

My cheeks burned, giving me away. Aida raised an eyebrow as a knowing smile slid across her mouth.

"Has it occurred to you that maybe he's been giving you space to figure out your own thoughts? You crushed on Tyler for *years*. What guy thinks he stands a chance against that?"

I gaped.

Could that really be it?

Aida shook her head. "Lainey, Lainey. You have it bad for him, don't you?"

"Maybe," I whispered.

Aida snorted. "Come here. You have a man to impress. Bring the rest of the sparkly hair pins."

An hour later, my hair was pinned, spritzed, and really did look fantastic. I had to hand it to Aida. She knew what she was about when it came to curling and accessorizing. I tugged self-consciously at the bottom of my sweater. It was an ugly sweater holiday party held at the local coffee shop and put on by one of the service organizations on campus. It wasn't the typical boozy sorority/fraternity affair, and I was glad for a quieter evening, even though there was Christmas music and already plenty of people milling about the cozy shop as Aida and I stepped over the threshold.

Roasted coffee and scents of cinnamon and nutmeg tickled my nose, and I took a generous inhale. The breath froze in my lungs as I caught sight of a familiar dark head of shaggy hair across the room. He turned, his lips pulled up in a full smile as he laughed at something Macy Taylor said.

Jealousy flooded my system and for a second, green hazed my vision.

I was saved from my sudden bout of envy as Josh Clark swung an arm around Macy's shoulders and she leaned into him.

"Mm-hmm. Don't think I didn't see that display of possessiveness there, Lainey Rowan," Aida whispered smugly. I willed my cheeks not to ignite. "Tonight is the night," she continued in a whisper. "I am not letting you back in the dorm room until you have a *chat* with lover boy."

"Aida!" I hissed her name.

She lifted a saucy eyebrow and nodded subtly toward Keiran.

Just as I risked a glance in his direction, Keiran turned and saw us. His face lit with a smile and my heart went pitter-pat as my belly dropped to my toes. I swallowed. Aida waved as naturally as anything while she threatened out the side of her mouth, "Remember, if you want to sleep in your bed with your blankets tonight, you will speak to him. Otherwise, I will pitch your favorite pillow and your comforter out the window." She winked at me, and I elbowed her.

"Am I interrupting something?" Keiran asked, glancing between us as he sauntered next to me.

"Nope," I said quickly. Probably too quickly.

"I'm going to go get a coffee. Anyone want anything?" Aida smiled, showing all her teeth.

"I'm good," Keiran said, lifting a red and green Styrofoam cup with a lid.

"I'll get you something, Lainey. You go have a good time." Aida patted my arm and moseyed to the counter.

"Um, hey," I stuttered as we were left alone but for the sea of people around us.

"Hey," Keiran said with a grin. "I like your hair that way." He took a casual sip of his coffee. Cinnamon wafted from him.

My heart thumped erratically in my chest. Aida's words echoed in my head. My own wild emotions crashed erratically against my ribs. A blush stole up my cheeks. This wouldn't do.

"That's a hideous sweater," I blurted, totally addled.

Keiran laughed. "It was the ugliest thing I could find." It was some monstrosity, likely from the sixties. A crocheted number done up in eye-searing hues of yarn with a Christmas tree made up of pom-poms on the front. "Hey. You're not laughing. What's wrong?" His whole attention suddenly focused on me.

My mouth was dry. I swallowed. "Can I talk to you?"

A flash of surprise followed by a millisecond of panic dashed across his face. "Sure." His voice was enviably steady.

Couples milled around us, music filling in any hope of quiet. "Not here," I said.

He nodded and tossed his coffee cup in a nearby trash can. "Come on." He grabbed the tips of my fingers, leading me through the throng of people and toward the back of the shop.

He'd held my hand like this countless times over the years, but it had never felt so questioning, so unsure, so tenuous.

Keiran led us into a hallway back by the restrooms but then opened a door that said STAFF ONLY and pulled me through. "Bobby owes me a favor. He won't mind if we talk up here." We went up a short flight of stairs to a narrow hallway, shadowed with low light and scents of the holiday. A quiet hush descended as the sounds of the party dimmed, leaving us cocooned in a soft hum of background music and muted voices.

He stopped, leaning against the wall, turned to face me. He started to let go of my fingers, but I gripped them hard. His eyebrows shot up into the dark thatch of hair flopped across his forehead. His fingers tightened around mine.

I groped for the right words, but none came. My gaze skittered around, landing anywhere but on Keiran's face. Instead of finding anything helpful, they grazed across the ceiling and a little clump of white waxy flowers and green leaves.

"Oh my gosh, it's mistletoe." I couldn't take the words back once they were out of my mouth.

Keiran glanced up at the little plant we were stopped directly under. A slow smile spread over his lips as his eyes tracked back to my face. His thumb rubbed over the back of my hand, and he shoved off the wall, taking a step into my space.

My heart thundered as I looked into Keiran's dark eyes, hypnotized by the sudden emotion I found there. The corners of his eyes crinkled, his expression both shy and wanting. He took one step more so that we were all but touching. His gaze trained to my lips and his Adam's apple bobbed. His eyes trailed back up my face until they met mine once more. For a charged moment, we held suspended, locked in a bubble of anticipation, hope, and uncertainty.

Keiran swallowed again. "Lainey, stop me if this isn't what you want."

But it was.

And then he kissed me.

This is the epitome of a Sweet kiss. The focus is all on the emotions, and there is very little physical description of what is taking place. However, if some slight description is added to the kiss, it can serve to heighten the tension, even though Keiran and Lainey are still sharing a sweet kiss.

The added description will use more sensory words and the feelings those physical sensations evoke. Because humans are multi-dimensional creatures, it's difficult to separate physical sensations from the emotional responses that are tied to them, particularly where romance and hormones are concerned.

In a romantic encounter, all of the five senses are involved. Using those five senses to process what a character is experiencing can be a powerful tool in helping your reader connect and feel what the character is feeling.

What do they see?

What do they hear?

What can they smell?

What are they feeling against their skin or beneath their fingertips?

Are they tasting anything?

Go to the next page and practice writing a brief sweet moment of swoon between your characters. After that, we'll move on to the next level on the thermostat, *swoony*.

Sweet Heat

♥

Swoony

Swoony Romance contains romantic tension. There is kissing. There is noticing. There may be some light physical descriptions. There is still an emphasis on feelings and emotions.

Swoony

Swoony Romance contains romantic tension. There is kissing. There is noticing. There may be some light physical descriptions. There is still an emphasis on feelings and emotions, but there should be more *physical* description in the swoony level of kissing. That way, tension is built up more so the reader and character release hits a little harder when the culmination finally happens. The climax has bigger impact.

Let's look at that last scene again with some more descriptors, taking this kiss from *Sweet* to *Swoony*. This slight adding of description builds the level and intensity.

"Oh my gosh, it's mistletoe."

Keiran glanced up, seeing the little plant we were stopped directly under. A slow smile spread over his lips as his eyes tracked back to my face. His thumb rubbed over the back of my hand. The heat of his body was searing as he shoved off the wall and took a single step into my space. He smelled like Christmas and possibilities.

My heart thundered as I looked into Keiran's dark eyes, hypnotized by the sudden emotion I found there. His brows drew together as the corners of his eyes crinkled, his expression both shy and wanting. He shuffled one more half step so that we were all but touching. His gaze trained to my lips as his Adam's apple bobbed.

His free hand slowly reached up, and his calloused fingertips grazed my jaw, his pinky sliding against my neck. A shiver worked down my spine as every one of my nerve endings ignited.

"Lainey, stop me if this isn't what you want." His throaty whisper ghosted skitters of excited trepidation over my shoulders.

His head inched toward me.

This wasn't how I'd planned things, but I knew without doubt that this was definitely what I wanted.

I wanted Keiran. My best friend. The boy who'd seen me and the man I now saw before me.

My palm braced against his chest, his heart thundering under my fingertips, and I raised up to my tip toes to be closer to his lips.

With aching slowness, he leaned down, and his mouth brushed against mine.

We held suspended in our own bubble, lips touching, souls knitting, promise budding in our perfect Christmas kiss.

This is still a gentle kiss, but by adding more sensory details and tying them to the emotions experienced alongside them, this builds swoon, heat, and overall romantic tension.

Let's look at a few more examples of tying emotion to sensory details. Think about how the first example in each pair compares to the second.

His lips brushed against mine.

His lips brushed against mine, **and heat exploded inside my chest**.

Her fingers trailed over the taut muscles in my forearm.

Longing like I'd never experienced unleashed inside me as her fingers trailed over the taut muscles in my forearm.

I inhaled, and the scent of cotton candy filled my nose. My lips closed over her mouth, and I tasted the sweet confection.

I inhaled the scent of cotton candy, **the smell unlocking memories we'd made together as children**. Wanting to keep not only those memories, but to make every future memory with her, my lips closed over hers, **and the sweet flavor of memory and sugar burst on my tongue**.

There are lots of ways to tie sensory details, memories, emotions, and even physical responses together in unique and stunning combinations to evoke emotion, swoon, and enjoyment in your readers as they devour the romance you've created between your characters.

Flip the page and jot down things you noticed that were different about the *Swoony* scene vs. the *Sweet* scene.

Steamy

Steamy Romance contains definite romantic tension. There is kissing; it might be descriptive. There is certainly noticing. There may be some more physical descriptions. There is still a large emphasis on feelings and emotions.

Steamy

Steamy Romance contains *definite* romantic tension. It's palpable and tangible. It's an action scene. There is still a large emphasis on feelings and emotions, but it's backdropped by physical action and response. There is kissing; It's probably *descriptive* kissing. There is certainly noticing. There are more physical descriptions. There are both more nouns and more adjectives. Deeper physical and emotional questions are asked and answered—like why are they enjoying this beyond just feeling good? A typical pattern in steamy kissing is two or three physical beats followed by an emotional explanation or response.

If the previous scene was to take a *steamy* turn, more physical description would be added to the kiss itself—to both the emotional *and* the physical responses.

"Oh my gosh, it's mistletoe."

Keiran glanced up, seeing the little plant we were stopped directly under. A slow smile spread over his lips as his eyes tracked back to my face. His thumb rubbed over the back of my hand, sending skitters of fire up my arm. The heat of his body was searing as he shoved off the wall and took a single step into my space. He smelled like Christmas and possibilities. Every cell in my body was attuned to him.

My heart thundered as I looked into Keiran's dark eyes, hypnotized by the sudden emotion I found there. His brows drew together, eyes crinkled at the edges, his expression both shy and wanting. His pupils widened as his gaze danced over my face. His pulse pounded up the side of his neck. My heart beat like a drum against my breastbone as heat kindled in my middle. Keiran shuffled one more half step so that we were all but touching. Electricity crackled in the scant space between us. His gaze trained to my lips as his Adam's apple bobbed.

His free hand slowed reached up and his calloused fingertips grazed my jaw, his pinky sliding against my neck. A shiver scraped down my spine as every one of my nerve endings ignited.

He swallowed again, desire plainly written across his face. Every longing he'd managed to keep trapped inside was now fully visible, laid bare in his brown eyes. A resonant ache welled inside me and the sudden intensity of my own want forced a gasp from my lips.

His gaze crashed into mine, sparks igniting the air around us.

"Lainey, stop me if this isn't what you want." His throaty whisper ghosted skitters of excited trepidation over my shoulders.

His head inched toward me.

I wanted Keiran. Wanted his lips against mine. Wanted him to want me like I wanted him. My best friend. The boy who'd seen me and the man saw me still. The man I saw in return.

My palm braced against his chest, his heart thundering under my fingertips, and I raised up to my tip toes to be closer to his lips. My chest brushed against his as his hand slid into the hair at the back of my head.

With aching slowness, he leaned down, and his lips brushed against mine. Softly, asking for permission.

My hand fisted into his shirt, both pulling myself toward his lips and him against me. His lips met mine, harder, and I melted under their pressure. My other hand slid across his shoulder, bracing against the bulge of his bicep underneath his hideous sweater. His fingers splayed against the curve of my waist and a whisper of a whimper echoed in the back of my throat.

How had I ever thought of Keiran as only a friend?

Without meaning to, my lips parted, and the tip of his tongue wisped against my bottom lip. Fire raced down my limbs as he woke hidden places inside me.

We held suspended in our own bubble, lips searching, tongues tangling, souls knitting, promise budding between us.

Something to note about steamy kissing or steamy swoon—one way to immediately up the heat level is to include the tongue. The tongue is an unassuming little organ of the body that can cause the greatest ecstasy or the utmost agony. With the tongue, a character can utter words of love, encouragement, of forgiveness, or they can deliver a crushing sentence of betrayal, hate, or death.

The tongue can also be used to heat a scene up *quickly*.

Giving description to what the tongue is doing will immediately ratchet up the tension and the passion.

The tongue can:
Moisten lips
Deepen a kiss
Taste
Plunge
Explore
Sweep
Slip
Part lips

Can you think of other descriptors the tongue can do?

Reread the three scenes—sweet, swoony, and steamy. Use the graphic organizer to jot down some of the differences you noticed. How did the tension escalate? Can you find some of the emotional and physical descriptors indicative of each level of swoon?

In order to better understand the different levels of swoon, we need to understand physical and emotional attraction. There's also science involved.

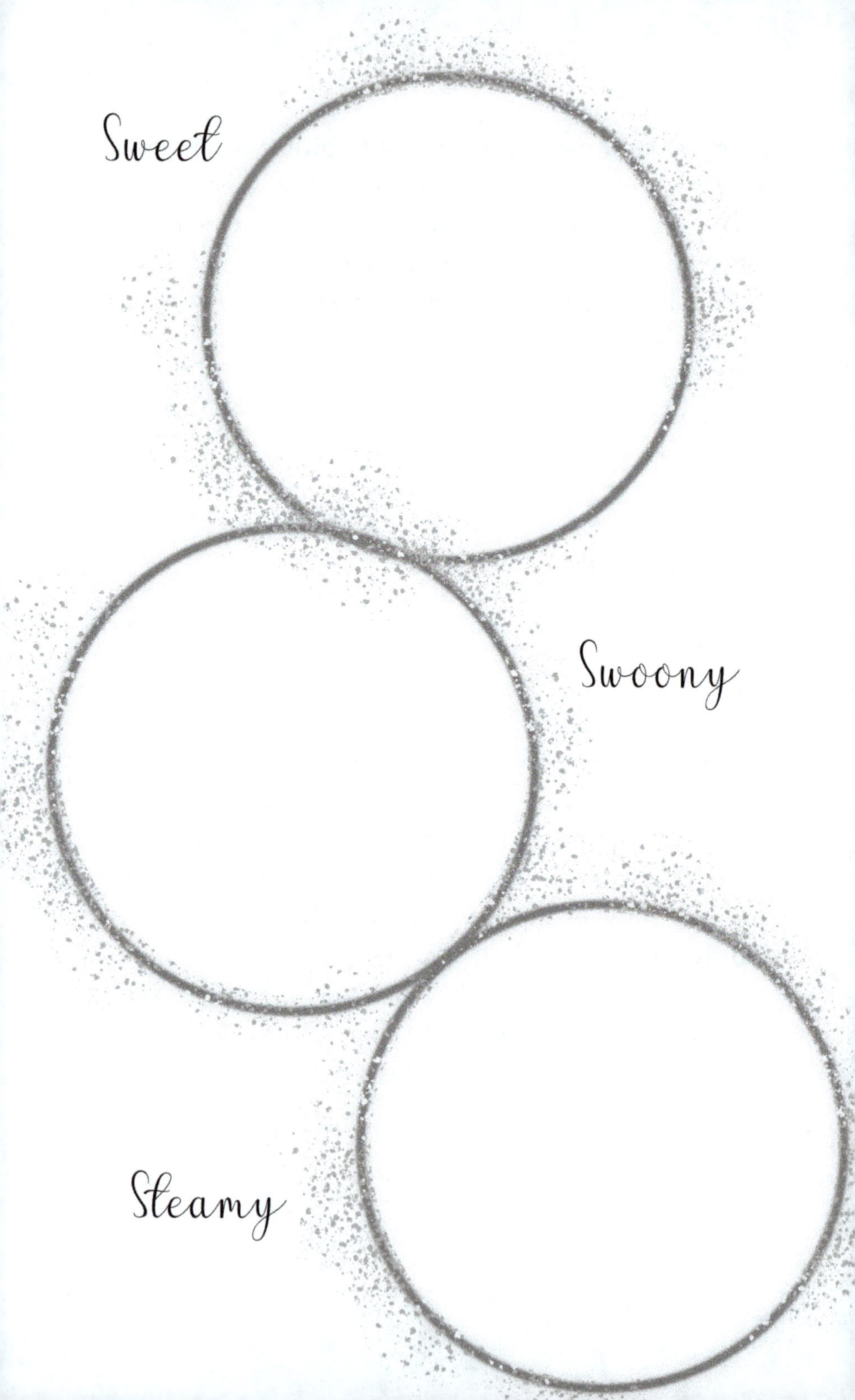

Sweet
Swoony
Steamy

THE SCIENCE OF KISSING

The Science of Kissing

Humans have five basic senses:

Hearing
Sight
Taste
Touch
Smell

All of these senses are actively involved when a romantic encounter occurs. Descriptions engaging multiple senses can dramatically heighten the swoon factor of a character's kiss.

How does the brush of fingers feel? Does the skin get hot? Does the character get goosebumps? What does the love interest smell like? Has he shaved? Does he have a five o'clock shadow that prickles? Is he attracted to the scent of her shampoo?

Some basic questions to ask yourself about the five senses:

Hearing
Does the breathing increase?
Is there a sharp inhale?
Are there breathy noises?

Is there other noise somewhere in the vicinity?

Is there mood music?

Sight

What is the character attracted to about the other?

What color are the eyes they're staring into?

Does she have lipstick on?

What are they wearing?

What do they see in the environment?

Do the things they might otherwise see fade away in the face of the romantic interest?

Taste

Did one of the characters recently eat something?

Did they drink something?

Do they taste of chocolate?

Does a character want to taste the other's lips?

Does a character kiss the other's fingers and taste the orange they just peeled?

Touch

What does the other character feel like?

Are they well muscled?

Are they pressed against a chest?

Can the character feel the other's heartbeat against the palm of their hand?

Does the romantic interest's touch bring goosebumps?

Does the scalp prickle with awareness?

Smell

What shampoo does the character use?

Do they have a natural scent?

Have they been near a fire?

Is there a specific smell on the romantic interest's breath?

Is there perfume or cologne?

Is there another scent in the vicinity that heightens awareness?

All of these physical senses can have emotional triggers or responses. Think of the smell of your favorite meal. Does it have any memories attached to it? Does it make you think of someone who makes it for you? A restaurant with fond memories? What about a specific perfume? Does your brain have any associations with roses? With the sight of the ocean?

The senses and what a character experiences through them in an emotional encounter will have a profound impact on the reader.

Now for more science. When a person is kissed by someone he or she is romantically interested in, there are typically several physiological responses that occur.

There may be anxiety involved (cortisol and adrenaline are often released). Body parts may sweat (especially palms and arm pits, but arm pits are generally less romantic than other areas). Blood pressure escalates (pupils may dilate). This causes the heart to pump faster (the heart thumps). The lungs draw more oxygen (may induce panting or ragged breathing).

Other chemicals are often released into the bloodstream as well—chemicals associated with happiness and pleasure and that often cause a craving for more of the pleasurable sensation (chemicals such as dopamine, oxytocin, and serotonin—the "happy cocktail" of hormonal chemicals).

When physical senses, physiological response, and emotions are all twisted together and presented on the page, it creates the perfect trifecta for swoon.

Look at the next few pages and see if you can add any of your own swoony words that might be helpful to reference the next time you're writing a swoony scene. Employ a thesaurus if you like.

The Five Senses

 Touch

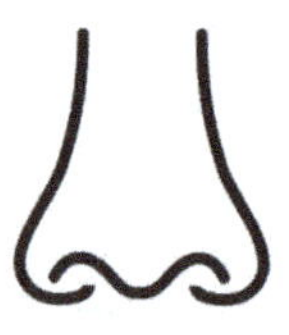 Smell

 Hearing

 Tasting

 Seeing

Hands

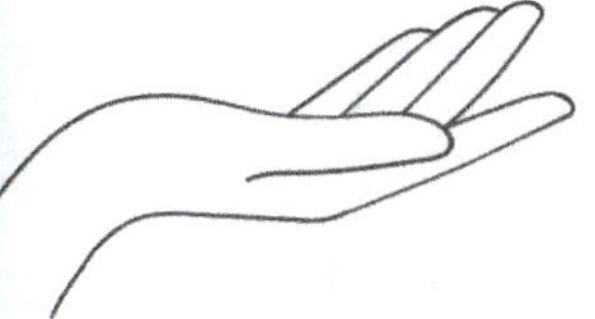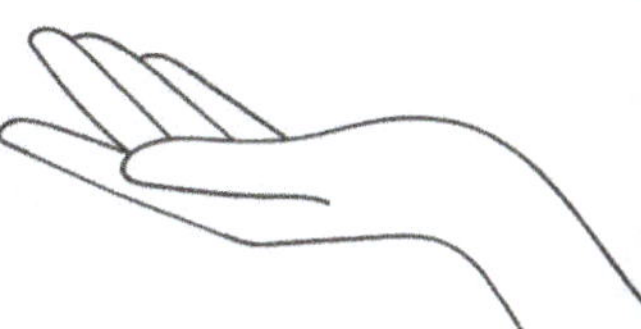

Stroke

Caress

Grasp

Clutch

Crush

Grope

Brush

Feather

Cradle

List some
other things
hands could
do:

Skin

Goosebumps

Tingle

Flush

React

Glisten

Damp

Sweat

Prickle

Awareness

List some other ways skin reacts:

Eyes

Flash

Snap

Sparkle

Glint

Assess

Rove

Follow

Gleam

Know

Vulnerable

Hooded

Darken

Dilate

Widen

Surprise

List some other things eyes do:

Ears

Moan

Groan

Gasp

Growl

Cry

Grunt

Whimper

Whisper

Shout

Shriek

Vocalize

Rumble

Husky

Panting

List some other things ears might hear:

Nose 

Inhaled

Scent

Musk

Floral

Specific scent

tied to a

specific

character

Flared

Bumped

Tapped

List some
other things
the nose
might
discover:

Hips

Twitch

Grind

Pressed

Thrust

Oscillate

Flush Against

Smashed

Swiveled

Gyrated

Moved

Hands on Hips

Jut

List some
other things
about hips:

Lungs

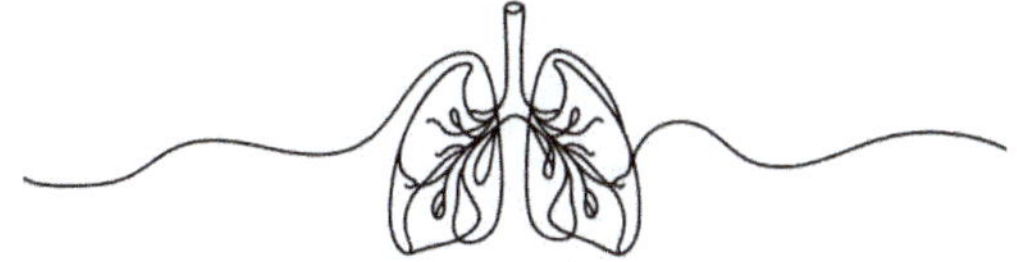

Gasp

Sucked in

Panting

Stutter

Forced Exhale

Sharp Inhale

Shallow

Tight

Painful

List some other ways lungs impact romance:

Neck

Curve of the neck

Base of the throat

Vein pulsing

Lean back

Neck/throat exposed

Pillar or Column of the throat

List some other ways to describe the neck:

THE
AFTER KISS

The After Kiss

There is also fall out once characters kiss. This can be positive or negative but shouldn't be ignored. A kiss changes the chemistry between the two characters; there is *always* a reaction.

Possible character reactions beside euphoria can include:

Apathy (Why are these characters kissing? Is it an arranged or dead marriage? Are they kissing only for the benefit of those watching?)

Joy (The typical, happy response.)

Excitement (Think of all those racing emotions and chemical reactions.)

Horror ("What have I just done?")

One-sided fears ("Did I do it right?")

Doubt ("Should I have kissed him/her? Did I rush the friendship? What if I just damaged our relationship beyond repair?")

Fear (Is this a trigger for your character because of past trauma? Are they aware of that past trauma, or is it a blind reaction?)

Sometimes all characters want is a second kiss. Other times, guilt can be the result. How does the kiss between the characters serve to move the plot forward?

The Kiss can be a good place to end a chapter and keep the reader engaged straight into the next—because they crave that After Kiss result.

Also, continue to add physical beats even in the After Kiss—heart rates are still increased and can be felt, seen in the pulse, or heard in a character's own head.

A good kiss, a well-placed kiss, will *impact* the story.

Think about your characters. How would they react to The Kiss? Remember to include both characters' reactions—even if it's in first person point of view, Character A will still see the reactions Character B is having and should note those, either in dialogue, or in internal thoughts.

Answer these questions: How has this kiss changed each character? Their thoughts? The story? How does the kiss move the plot forward?

Read this excerpt from the first chapter of LOST SHIFT. Katie and Donovan are werewolves with a tangled past. They live in the contemporary world, but simultaneously exist in their werewolf society. This is an example of an early kiss that does not have all the swoony, happy after glow between the characters. It's laced with guilt and what–ifs.

Donovan

My chest was tight. Tight like when my mom died. Too tight. Like I couldn't breathe because the walls were caving in on me. Only, there were no literal walls. Just the darkness, the forest, the trees, the stars shining softly above the dark canopy as I leaned my head against the cool glass of the truck window. Just metaphorical walls and my gloom threatening to crush me.

I hadn't realized how hard leaving Rock Falls without Sarah would be. I wasn't sorry I'd given her up—she was in love with Cade, and he was in love with her. But I think a tiny part of me had been falling for her, too. And coming home from the Lacessere empty handed, without her Alpha genes to mix with mine, left me feeling hollow. Somehow less. Like I wasn't enough.

"Hey, snap out of it, Donovan," Angus, my older cousin, said as he mock punched my shoulder. "What's going on in that head of yours? You've been quiet the whole way back. And it's been a *long* drive from Delaware back home to Oregon."

I grimaced ruefully. "Sorry, Angus. Just thinking."

"Yeah. I bet." Angus snorted and rubbed his neck. The faintest markings of bruises where Cade had his incisors against his throat during the last challenge still lingered. "Are you sorry you gave her up?" He wasn't condemning my choice, but I could hear his curiosity.

"No." I sighed. "If I'd forced her hand and we'd become mates, it would have just festered between us." I shook my head. "She couldn't love me."

"She respects you. That wasn't enough?"

I sighed and my breath fogged up the window. "No. Not when you love someone like she loves Cade." It had been written on every inch of her once I won the Lacessere—the challenge for her hand. Her look of horror, tinged even with revulsion, when I won the right to Claim her, marry her, be her mate and join our would-be Alpha bloodlines, was burned into my brain. My skin crawled thinking about it.

I'd given her up. I had no claim on her now—never would again. I didn't regret what I'd done, but my confidence had taken a serious hit. For the first time in a long time, I felt unsure of myself.

Who was I?

"Donovan! Angus! You're back. I wasn't sure I should expect you before tomorrow," Dad, Alpha of the extensive Hazelton werewolf pack, called from the doorway, the porch light glinting off his silvering hair.

"Hey, Dad," I said as I dragged myself from the truck, unfolding my stiff joints.

Dad met us at the bottom of the steps and gave me a quick hug. "Welcome home, son." He cupped my jaw in his weathered hand, giving my cheek a fatherly pat. "I've had a Gathering organized for tomorrow night to welcome you home properly with the whole pack." He smiled at me, though there was a touch of sadness in his expression. Some emotion I couldn't identify slithered through my gut, curdling like shame, but leaving a hollowness behind.

"Thanks," I croaked.

Dad squeezed my shoulder. "Angus, we'll see you tomorrow then?"

"Sure thing, Uncle Hal. I'm going to get myself home to Emma." I could see the sparks in my cousin's eyes from where I stood by the house. A thread of jealousy wormed into the uncomfortable mass in my belly. Angus and Emma had Claimed each other last spring. They'd been nearly intolerable in their ardor for each other since then. Sarah flashed across my brain. Wolf raised his head wearily inside me.

"See you, Angus," I said, waving tiredly and shoving the thoughts from my head. I had no energy for anything more than falling into bed.

My dad, as Alpha, had planned an epic party to welcome me back home—I think he'd planned on welcoming his future daughter-in-law along with me, but that hadn't worked out. I needed to marry someone with Alpha or Beta genes to keep the pack bloodlines strong. Girls with Alpha or Beta genes were few and far between. Giving Sarah up would be seen as a colossal loss to some. I sighed. My mom had been the cousin of a Beta. I wished she were still alive to offer some advice in the girl department. I shook off the sadness that came with thoughts of my mom. Werewolves married and mated young. There wasn't an expiration date on when I had to find the girl to carry my genes into the next generation, but at nineteen, I was expected to find that girl in the not-too-distant future.

I was not in the mood for a Gathering. But now that I'd been home all of twelve hours, I was expected to get back out and mingle with my pack.

"Donovan! It's dusk! Are you coming down?" Dad called up the stairs. I sighed again, glancing out my window into the forested twilight beyond the panes.

"Yeah." I swallowed, collecting my courage, trying to ignore the ache in my chest, and headed down the stairs.

By the time I got to the Gathering, the bonfire was lit and everyone in the pack had heard the heroically spun tale of how I'd given up Sarah and her Alpha bloodline so she could be with the wolf she loved.

"That took a lot of guts, Donovan, giving up the girl like that," a friendly older pack member said as he clapped me on the back.

"I'm not sure I would have," another said with a smile and a swig of his soda. My insides crawled.

"I think he did the right thing. It's rare enough for Alphas and Betas to find love early if they aren't true mates. Donovan will always be the hero of that story," a woman called from the shadows.

I smiled politely at it all, responding when I had to, but retreating into myself as the night lengthened and shadows darkened the clearing. Once darkness fell completely, and I was less likely to be missed, I melted into the fringe, letting those around the bonfire tell jokes and stories. I felt like an outsider in my own pack. I'd never felt this way before. It rocked me to my core, leaching concern and trepidation into my normally healthy confidence.

Watching alone from the shadows calmed my heart but still left my insides bruised and unsure.

"Van." The soft-spoken word had me wheeling around. I hadn't heard Katie's quiet footfalls over the newly sprouted covering on the forest floor. My heart plummeted, hoping I could escape detection here in the trees, but as she came close, her eyes shined at me in a way that made my stomach dip.

"Hey, Katie," I said, my voice hushed. She came over to me, just inside the borders of my personal space, the moonlight filtering down weakly on her red-black hair only to be swallowed up in large red-brown eyes.

"I hear you made quite the sacrifice back in Rock Falls," she said lightly, her voice betraying nothing. My insides churned. Though her voice gave nothing away, her eyes did. She drank me in, mystery and desire swirling together in the deep pools of her dark cinnamon gaze.

Life sparked inside the dead void of my chest. Feeling returned to my limbs. The pressure in my chest eased enough I drew a full breath as I watched her. Looking at her, I felt *something*. I knew she'd be willing. She'd been half in love with me since the night we found her, bleeding and alone, her pack slaughtered by feral wolves so many years ago. She'd looked at me then with something akin to hero-worship, but as we'd grown older, it had morphed into something infinitely more dangerous.

She was beautiful. Beautiful and alluring. I'd never felt anything beyond friendship for Katie...but looking at her, longing for *something* welled up inside my chest. Any sense I had fled. I took a step closer. Her eyes widened. Her heartbeat picked up, echoing faintly in my ears. My own sped up to match. For just a second, Sarah's pale face, her celery green eyes and light blonde hair superseded Katie's darker looks. I blinked. We were inches from each other. Her fiery-sweet scent of allspice and maple invaded my senses and my blood pumped quicker. My gaze tracked to her mouth. Her lips parted as she inhaled quickly.

Willing the lump in my chest to beat again, to rid myself of the doubt that clung to me closer than my fur, I lowered my face to hers, my lips covering hers as my hands slid around her waist, drawing her flush against me. Wolf jerked inside me.

A shocked, guttural noise sounded in her chest. For one charged second, she stood stock-still against me, but as my lips moved slowly against hers, she melted into my chest, her mouth responding in a way that made my knees weak. Her hands dragged up my biceps to twine around my neck. For long moments, we kissed. The darkness inside me abated as her body pressed against me, as my hands followed the curve of her waist to the small of her back, up to her shoulders, pulling her closer.

I kissed her harder, craving the spark she ignited inside me, the way kissing her made me feel. She groaned softly against my mouth, her hands twisting into the hair at the base of my neck as she went up on tip toes, her chest pressing against mine. The hair on my arms stood on end. Her muffled noise carried so much longing, so much want, that it snapped me out of my trance. My lips froze against hers, my hands stilling where they gripped her sides.

Wait.

Why was I kissing Katie?

Was I kissing Katie? I was thinking about Sarah.

Was...was I *using* her?

Wolf and I recoiled at the realization that it was exactly what I was doing.

Using her unwittingly for my own selfish pleasure without a single thought of what I was doing to her. My stomach heaved as I tore my lips from hers, crashing a step back into the underbrush. My heart pounded as I panted, desperately trying to drag air into my frozen lungs. In horror, I watched numbly as she blinked once. Twice. Then her eyes filled with tears, and she fled.

I was the worst kind of dog alive.

This is an example of consequences of a kiss also of the sort of kiss that breeds complication for the characters to overcome as the story progresses.

Now read this excerpt from A MURDER ONCE FORGOTTEN. This is a kiss laced with uncertainty, but of a different variety. It, too, provides complications, but the resolution is driven by vulnerability and compassion, rather than guilt and lust.

ELLERY

The ride to Connor's house was quiet and uneventful. My brain twisted around and around the past hour, trying to work out what I should do.

"Home sweet home," Connor said as we pulled into his driveway. It was snowing in earnest now, the white flakes coming down with a vengeance. We dashed up to his door, careful on the three steps leading up to it. Connor fumbled with the lock, taking two tries to get the key in before handing it to me. "It'll be quicker if you just do it," he quipped.

"Sure." I unlocked the door, and he ushered me inside with a hand to my back. His house was warm and cheery. He flipped a switch, and a beautiful Christmas tree lit up with color. It pulled at something inside me—his house, though he was a bachelor, was decorated for Christmas. Garlands and sparkly tinsel decorated the mantle and looped across the curtain rod of the large window at the far end of the room. A nativity scene was set out on an end table and big glass ornaments hung from various points about the room.

Connor grinned sheepishly. "I know, it's a bit much. Jana and Morey came over on one of my days off and declared they were going to get my house ready for the season. Well, Jana did the declaring. Morey put tinsel on every possible surface." An expression of sheer adoration covered his face.

"They did a wonderful job." A smile tugged at my lips as I thought about having family like that to come alongside me. I knew my parents loved me. But it had been difficult to be close to them ever since we'd left Pine Tree Hollow. There was always an underlying current of tension.

"Make yourself at home. I'm going to go find my glasses." He gently ran his hand over my upper arm and disappeared down a hallway that probably led to bedrooms.

I came into the room, gently draping my coat over the back of his couch, taking my time to let my gaze linger. It wasn't a huge house, but it was homey. It felt warm. I wandered into the kitchen, separated from the living room by a partial wall. There was a big window over the sink, and on the ledge was a picture of Jordan, me, and Connor at the lake when we were teenagers. It might have even been the same trip that someone had snapped the picture of me that Grandma had sitting in her windowsill at her house. I glanced out at the falling snow. The world was turning white, and for a brief flash, I pictured myself standing at this very sink. Doing dishes after having dinner with Connor. Cuddling on the couch. Watching a movie and having hot chocolate together. Loving him. I stepped away and sagged against the wall.

I blew out a ragged breath.

"Ellery? Where'd you go? Oh. Here you are. You okay?" Connor, replacement glasses resting on his nose, and handsome as ever, leaned against the half wall bracketing the kitchen.

"I want to date you," I blurted.

Connor's eyebrows rose to his hairline. "Come again?"

"I want to date you," I whispered.

Connor slowly closed the distance between us.

"You want to date me?" Hope lit his eyes. Connor's arms carefully bracketed my head, his palms flat on the wall behind me, in my space, but not touching me. I both yearned for his touch and was terrified of it. I wanted him to touch me. To hold me. To want me.

But those same thoughts sent my heart into overdrive as the panic that hadn't surfaced earlier tingled in my fingers now.

"Ellery," he said softly, voice rough. "You're shaking." His gaze roamed over my face. "Why?"

"Because I'm scared," I whispered.

His eyebrows climbed his forehead before drawing to-gether. "Scared of me? Scared of dating me?"

I shook my head. "I'm scared of letting anyone get close enough to care about them."

We were silent a moment as tears stung the back of my eyes. I blinked them away.

"I'm already that close, aren't I?" His brown eyes were infinitely gentle and kind.

I broke the contact, glancing down, shocked to find my hands fisted into the material of his t-shirt. I heaved a breath, hating the tears that welled again at the back of my eyes.

"Yeah. And that terrifies me." My words were barely audible. "The last time I let someone get that close, it left me with scars. Big, fat, ugly emotional scars."

Slowly, he slid one hand from the wall and carefully let his fingers trail from my jaw to my chin, tipping it up so he could see my eyes once more.

"I'm not scared. And I'm not going anywhere." His thumb grazed over my chin. "Can I tell you something?"

I nodded.

"Ellery, I've had a crush on you since I was a scrawny fifteen-year-old and you were a perfect, blonde dream standing at the edge of the dock, staring out at the water, with the wind blowing your hair back. That picture over your grandma's sink? That was the exact moment I think I fell for you." His eyes flicked to the picture on his own windowsill. "That trip to the lake was defining for me." A soft smile tilted his lips.

A flush crawled up my cheeks and I couldn't stop the grin that tugged at my mouth. "Really?"

"Mm–hmm." It rumbled deep in his chest, vibrating through my fingertips that were now pressed against him, having released their strangle hold on his shirt.

"And...you still have a crush on me?" I whispered.

"Well, I'd say it's a little more serious than a crush now, but yeah. Yeah, I really, really do."

We stood there in a little bubble of our own, suspended in time, drinking each other in. My mind buzzed with possibilities. I was still nervous, but saying the words out loud had robbed them of some of their power. I'd been vulnerable and told Connor how messed up I was, and he hadn't even blinked. Acceptance and hope shone from his eyes. They flicked to my lips so quickly I almost missed it, but then he swallowed, and his Adam's apple bobbed. Heat spread in my middle.

The last boy I'd kissed had been Jason.

My belly flipped.

"That weekend at the lake—did you ever think about kissing me?" I couldn't believe the question left my mouth, but it had, and it hung there in the air between us.

Connor's eyes crinkled behind his glasses. "Probably more than was advisable. And not just that weekend at the lake." His fingers threaded into the hair at the base of my neck, thumb sweeping over my jaw.

"Do—do you still want to kiss me?" My voice was breathless. So was the rest of me. Excitement and trepidation were alternately numbing and tingling the ends of my fingers. I wanted the last memory of Jason's kiss gone. Replaced. By something far better, stronger, realer. Something I only wanted to share with Connor.

"Mm–hmm," he rumbled again. Light flared behind his eyes, waking something to life that called to me like a siren's song.

Any words I might have uttered fled, and I just stood there, back to the wall, Connor wrapped around me, shielding me from anything outside the bubble where we were cocooned together. My lips parted and my breath shortened.

"Kiss me," I whispered.

Connor searched my face. "You sure?" His voice was rough.

I nodded. He hesitated, then slowly—ever so slowly—dipped his head until our lips were only a breath apart, paused a moment longer, then with aching tenderness, brushed his lips against mine for a fraction of a second.

Air rushed from my lungs as his mouth left mine. My shoulders lost their rigidity and something that had been locked tight inside my chest for years released with a shaky breath. He searched my eyes again, and when I tipped my face to him, he stepped closer. His hand on the wall moved to rest lightly on my waist, his other sliding back along my jaw to cup my face. With the same beautiful agony as he did the first time, he slowly lowered his head.

My eyes slid shut as his lips touched mine again, brief as butterfly wings kissing in midair. His lips pressed just hard enough that I wanted to open my mouth. Before I could, he pulled back, his thumb running over my cheek once more.

"Amazing," he whispered.

Pleasant shivers raced from the crown of my head to the tips of my toes.

I lifted my face, indicating that I'd like him to kiss me again. My panic melted away, and in its wake, desire bloomed, soft and sweet.

He dipped once more, this kiss as brief as the others. I searched his face, unsure why he was stopping. I was happy to continue exploring his gentle kisses, unless he wasn't enjoying them. The thought curdled in my middle.

"I want to take this slow and do things the right way. I feel like I've waited half of forever for this one moment, and I don't want to rush it or do the wrong thing." He swallowed and relief smoothed the knots forming in my shoulders. "You are worth the wait." He smiled, eyes crinkling at the edges behind his glasses.

I was *worth the wait.*

CONNOR

I kissed Ellery McDaniels.

The woman I'd wanted to kiss for nearly a decade of my life.

The woman who hadn't kissed anyone since her high school boyfriend who had meant the world to her at one point.

Man, oh man, I hoped I was a better kisser than Jason. *Please let me be a better kisser than Jason!* My heart pounded against my ribs as endorphins and dopamine did the cha-cha together in my brain. I was both euphoric and as nervous as I had been the night of the party—the night I had wanted to tell her how I felt.

"What are you thinking?" Ellery asked softly. Her breath caressed the side of my face, and my knees might have actually quivered.

"I hope I'm a better kisser than Jason." The words blurted themselves from my mouth and as soon as they dropped into the air around us, I wanted to yank them back behind my teeth. Mortification was an unpleasant tang at the back of my throat. "I mean," I stuttered.

Ellery giggled. She *giggled*. Was that a good thing? She raised one pale brow and crooked her finger for me to lean down into the scant ten inches between us.

Of course, I did.

Her hand slid along the slight stubble on my jaw, cupping me just behind my ear. My heartbeat was as unsteady as my breathing. I was a touchy person, but nothing had prepared me for the lightning that ignited in my blood as Ellery's fingers intentionally moved across my skin. She tugged my head down near her lips, and I was utterly helpless to stop her.

Her lips ghosted the outside of my ear, and I wondered if I should brace a hand on the wall to keep myself from complete collapse, though if I did that, I'd have to take one of my hands off her, and I wasn't willing to do that either.

"You are definitely a better kisser than Jason." Her soft words were a delightful tickle against my ear and my entire chest heaved as relief, embarrassment, and maybe a hint of pride settled over my shoulders in a confusing, mostly pleasant mix.

"I'm glad to hear it," I said, wincing as my voice cracked.

I felt her smile before she gently kissed my cheek. My eyes glided closed as her lips lingered.

The consequences of The Kiss will impact future interactions between your characters. Remember, consequences can be good or bad, and sometimes both at the same time. Flip to the next page and write down any thoughts you have about the After Kiss.

List some possible consequences for the After Kiss
between your characters.

Structuring the Swoon

Over the next couple of pages, we're going to read a story and watch the break down of how the swoon is introduced and how it plays out in the story, *The Cadence of Christmas.*

But before that, remember, there are five main components any story needs to have proper swoon.

1. **Attraction**

2. **Emotion**

3. **Reaction**

4. **Vulnerability**

5. **Physical Action**

It's the combination of these things, in varying degrees, that achieves the different levels of swoon.

Attraction—attraction between characters is what gives readers those happy tingles. This can be emotional attraction or physical attraction. If Character A does not find Character B attractive in some estimation, then you cannot create swoon. Attraction can be physical or emotional, but both elements are necessary. Sometimes emotional attraction precedes physical attraction. Sometimes physical attraction leads to better understanding which then provides the catalyst of emotional attraction. Both physical and emotional attraction are needed for swoon.

Emotion—if a character is *only* physically attracted to another character, you cannot create swoon. You create a one-dimensional attraction based only on the outer appearance. When you create swoon, you're creating an emotional depth that draws the reader in and gives them an emotional fulfillment. Humans are multi-dimensional creatures, and their romances are, too. Romance in its entirety involves all parts of the body, inside and out.

Reaction—characters must react to the attraction and emotion of the other character. If there is no reaction to the attraction pull, there's no tension. Tension is what keeps your reader reading. Reactions can be physical or emotional or both. They're not always good, either. Sometimes there are several unfavorable reactions to attraction before there is a positive one. Think of tropes like enemies to lovers where there is often intense attraction and intense hatred at the beginning of the story. Sometimes it is only that intense physical attraction that saves a character's life long enough for the emotional pull to come into play.

Vulnerability—this is the biggest factor that sets swoony romance apart. When one character becomes vulnerable to the other, they open themselves up. It's risk. It's trust. It's hope. It's intoxicating. It's necessary to create swoon. Vulnerability breeds intimacy. Intimacy is something humans crave. There is no deeper relationship than the caring, vulnerable, intimate relationship between a pair of lovers. Fiction reflects reality, and characters should reflect these innermost desires as well.

Physical Action—the swooniest stories will have some sort of physical culmination in the romance. Depending on the heat level, these physical reactions can vary widely. Think of the infamous Austen "hand flex." Such a miniscule, innocent gesture that has had millions swooning dead away for literal centuries. Similarly, many swoony romances climax with kisses or comparable physical action. This physical action is not always displayed on the page either. Many fade to black or closed-door romances are epically swoony, but the physical actions don't need to be spelled out on the page for the reader. Imagination is plenty powerful.

These things don't need to be all crammed into one paragraph. There is an ebb and flow to how often each of these things is used, and part of it is dependent on author style, genre, and target audience. All of these elements should lead up to the physical action (usually, The Kiss). More on that later. For now, see if you can find these five elements in the following story.

Cadence's dreams are finally coming to fruition. She's just won the leading part in Nutcracker, The Alternate, the most prestigious production of the year at Archibald Academy. But not everyone is happy about it.

Struggling to get the complicated movements right, Cadence works for hours with her dance partner, Jordan. When she sees sparks flying between Jordan and her roommate, Cadence tries to set them up, vowing to practice on her own.

Relying on her best friend, Zane, to help her, Cadence finally finds confidence in herself. And finds an unexpected attraction to the boy who has been by her side for years.

All Cadence's hopes are crushed when she finds Zane kissing her arch-nemesis understudy. The night of the performance dawns and disaster strikes.

Will Cadence be able to trust Zane in a way she never has before?

The Cadence of Christmas is a sweet romance novella perfect for those who enjoy deep friendships, swoony first loves, and the magic of the holiday season.

The Cadence of Christmas

CADENCE

"Cadence? You up?"

Was I up? I hadn't been able to sleep for all the nerves until the wee hours, and now my eyeballs were cemented shut.

"Cadence?" It was Mina, a girl from two doors down the hallway. "Zane McAlister has been waiting outside the dorm, freezing his rear end off for at least the last ten minutes."

Poop.

My eyelids flew open, and I snatched my phone off my nightstand.

Yup. Three texts from Zane.

Coming! I quickly texted back, then leapt out of bed.

"Thanks, Mina. I'm up!"

"Sure thing. Wear your earmuffs. It's chilly." Her receding footsteps echoed lightly down the hallway. Channi's bed was empty, so I assumed she was already up and about. I should have had her make sure I was up.

I shoved my hair into a messy bun, threw on a sports bra, leggings, and a few other layers on top, and ran out the door. One quick stop at the bathroom, and I was out the door seven minutes after Mina's wake-up call.

"Wondered if you were coming at all," Zane said, blowing on his gloved hands, his green eyes twinkling. His dark hair flopped over his forehead, poking out from beneath his knit cap and disheveled perfectly in a way that made girls on campus swoon.

But not me. Zane had been my best friend since elementary school, and it was hard to swoon over the guy who purposely farted on you at his ninth birthday party. Swooning was out of the question. But best friend? Absolutely.

"Sorry I'm late. I didn't sleep well," I confessed.

"Too excited?" he asked, smiling, as we fell into step, jogging down the path from the girl's dormitory toward the athletic field. It was our ritual we did nearly every morning. While my other best friend and room-

Already, it's established that Zane is handsome, at least by the standards of some girls on campus.

This is still <u>Attraction</u>.

mate, Channi, punished herself on the elliptical, Zane and I braved the elements and ran through the campus's impressive, wooded paths. What Archibald School of the Arts lacked in modern convenience, cut off from the rest of the world in their isolated patch of glory in upstate New York, they made up for in their majestic campus.

"Terrified, nervous, excited; just want it to be over," I puffed, my breath pluming in a little white cloud.

"You're going to get a lead part. You're one of the best dancers at Archibald."

"I will absolutely die if Amy gets the part of Marie." I sighed, frigid air burning my lungs as we turned to go down the path deeper into the woods behind the athletic complex.

Zane chuckled beside me. I glared.

"What if Channi gets the part of Marie?" He glanced at me sideways, feet thumping rhythmically on the paved pathway.

I swallowed. "If Channi gets the part of Marie, I will be delighted for her."

"And?" he prompted.

"I'll still wish I would have gotten it, but I want Channi to get an invitation to Carmen as much as I want one. Hard to impress scouts when you're dressed as a chorus mouse or toy soldier."

"Carmen the only place you want to go?"

"They are renowned for producing principal ballerinas—my life's ambition. But I still need an invitation to the program. Still have to impress scouts at the final performance." I sucked in a frigid lung full of air. "And do that, I have to win one of the main parts."

Just thinking about it churned my guts into a mass of writhing snakes.

"Just breathe, Cady."

"Easy for you to say. You've already secured your spot behind the sound board." I groaned. "Is it eight o'clock yet?"

Their friendship establishes an Emotional connection.

Zane checked his watch. "Nope. Almost seven. Let's cut our run a little short, grab breakfast, and then you can try to unwind before checking the posting at eight."

He was always so logical. "I need coffee, but I'm afraid it's just going to make me more anxious."

"Come on." Zane was puffing some, too, now that we'd covered a good chunk of our normal run. "Let's sprint back to school and hit the cafeteria. I'm still cold."

"Deal." I took off like a shot, letting the chilly air wash over me in a cleansing wave.

My heart pounded as I tried to calm its racing. It was time. 7:55. Half the student body was crushed against either side of me. Channi gripped my hand hard enough to break my bones, her thick black braid mangled and twisted in her free fingers. Headmistress Greystoke seemed to float down the hallway; even her walk was graceful.

The List was in her hands.

Either my dreams would take flight, or shatter along with my heart at my feet.

My eyes were glued to Ms. Greystoke as she paced sedately, a coy smile playing at her lips as students parted like the Red Sea before her, leaving her way clear to the cork board mounted on the wall.

My pulse hammered through my head, thundering and throbbing through my temples. Black dots floated at the edge of my vision. *This was it. This was it. This was it.*

Ms. Greystoke reached the corkboard and twirled to face us, The List clutched to her chest. Her mellow voice rang out over the assembled students.

"Regardless of the names on this paper, all of you have worked hard this semester. But it's nothing compared to how hard you'll be working on this next piece. James Alderton will be flying in next week to teach the choreography for *Nutcracker, The Alternate*. As you read your names off on this list, remember that. It's two weeks until performance night. This will be a whirlwind like most of you have not experienced to this point in your young lives. But with those thoughts in mind, I won't keep you in suspense any longer." Her smiled tipped, the light catching on her iron-gray hair pulled back in a severe bun. She turned and pinned The List that would determine the rest of my life to the corkboard.

Students swarmed like a mass of fire ants, trying to get a look.

Amy Trent—my arch nemesis and stupidly talented dancer—headed the mob. She shrieked, and my blood pressure skyrocketed. I wasn't sure if it was a shriek of excitement or disappointment.

"Was that good or bad?" Channi asked as we cut off each other's circulation, gripping our hands together so hard it hurt.

"I don't know," I replied. The crush of bodies propelled us forward, students breaking upon The List like waves, finding their names and melting off to the sides.

We'd be in the next wave. Anxiety wrapped tentacles around my middle, squeezing the oxygen from my lungs. Zane caught my eye. He stood off to the side, well away from the herd, but there silently supporting me just the same. He nodded, lips tipped in a crooked smile meant to encourage me.

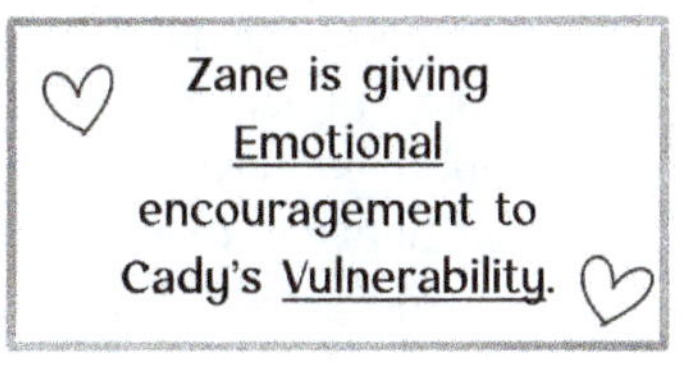

"This is it!" Channi whispered as we approached.

The List loomed, reaching claws into my soul and dragging me nearer, both repelling and attracting me to read its contents.

Panic hammered against my breastbone, and I thought I might pass out from the sheer number of nerves rattling through me.

Channi screamed beside me, nearly jerking my arm from its socket.

"I'm the Sugar Plum Fairy!" She squealed, drawing several congratulations and a few sneers from surrounding students.

My heart fluttered—if Channi was Sugar Plum, then there was only one other major role. And Amy might already have taken the part. Hardly daring to breathe, I found *Marie*, then followed the ellipses to a name.

My name.

I stared stupidly, tracing the letters C–A–D–E–N–C–E C–O–L–E with my eyes, trying to let the words soak in.

"Well?" Zane asked, shouldering his way through the crowd to stand behind me. Without thinking, I let my shoulders sink back against his chest. Suddenly overcome with complete relief, my heart stuttered, only to feel my pulse skyrocket in the next instant.

"I'm her. I'm Marie," I whispered.

Zane chuckled and dragged Channi and me off to the side. Suddenly, my limbs came to life like a firework exploded inside me. "Zane! Channi! I'm *her*!" I whisper-shrieked. I jumped up and down, yanking them both into a hug hard enough we all nearly knocked heads.

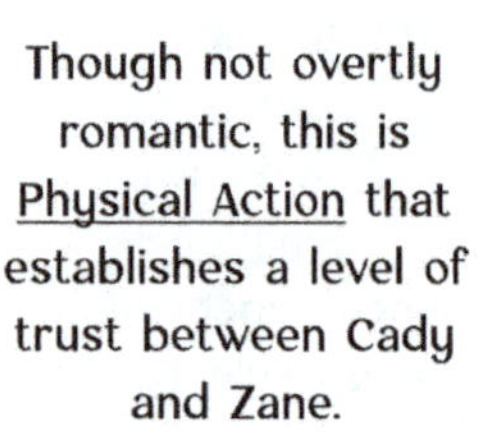

Zane laughed, looping an arm easily around my back and his other around Channi. "Congrats to both of you. You've got to call your parents. You know your mom has been on pins and needles all morning."

"Yes!" I dug my phone out of my pocket.

"It's too loud in here. I'm going to call outside," Channi said. "But congratulations! I'm so happy for you, Cadence!"

"Oh my gosh, you, too, Channi!" We hugged and squealed again as we wiggled in excitement through the doors to the commons, Zane tagging behind.

"Mom!" I shouted into the phone.

"What? What? Did they post parts? What did you get?" Mom's tone was just as excited as mine.

"I'm her! I'm *Marie*! I can't believe it!" I screeched excitedly into the phone.

Mom screamed her enthusiasm on the other line. "I knew you'd do it! I'm going to call your father as soon as we're off the line here. Honey, I'm so proud of you! We'll come up and take you out to dinner tonight to celebrate."

"I think I'm in shock," I confessed, rubbing a hand over my forehead, giddy inside.

"Well, at least it's the good kind of shock." Mom laughed. "Where do you want to go to celebrate?"

"Mmm, Ho Wang's. You know there's nothing better than their steamed fish in that yummy garlic sauce."

"If you say so." I heard Mom's smile through the phone. "Are Zane and Channi there, too?"

I glanced over my shoulder. Sure enough, Zane was there, smile still on his face, waiting for me to finish my call.

"As always. Channi is the Sugar Plum Fairy. It's surreal. It's *exactly* what we hoped for. And yes, Zane's here. I'll drag him with us tonight. I think Channi has that thing with her aunt's family tonight. One of her cousins is getting married."

"We'll pick you all up at five. Love you. I can't wait to watch you perform!"

"Love you, too. Thanks, Mom. See you guys tonight."

I ended the call and looked up at Zane.

"We're celebrating with dinner tonight!"

He chuckled. "I gathered. Congrats, Cady. I'm seriously proud of you."

All the bliss might make my head explode.

"Hey, Cadence. Looks like we'll be seeing a lot of each other." Jordan Hazlet sauntered past, biceps bulging beneath the tight fit of his athletic shirt. "Looking forward to being your Nutcracker prince." He winked as he continued down the hallway.

My eyebrows quirked up.

This ballet just got a lot more interesting.

ZANE

I was so stoked for Cady and Channi. They had worked their butts off, and I was glad things were paying off for them. I eyed Amy Trent as she flounced down the hall. I'd been close enough to the list to see that instead of getting a major part like Cady or Channi, Amy had been cast in several smaller roles. And was Cady's understudy. I hoped that didn't cause issues. Knowing Amy, she'd be sure to cause a ruckus about it regardless.

Zane has an <u>Emotional</u> reaction to Jordan's words. He also has a <u>Physical Reaction.</u> While these aren't directed at Cady, they are a direct result of the way Zane feels about her...and how Jordan might also feel about Cady.

"Hey, Cadence. Looks like we'll be seeing a lot of each other," Jordan said as he passed. Some internal alarm went off inside my head and I had to work to keep my lips over my teeth, lest I outright snarl at him.

He seemed like a nice enough guy from what I knew of him. We had a few classes together, but something about him just didn't sit well. I definitely didn't like the way his eyes slithered over Cady and then Channi.

Not at all.

And he was the Nutcracker prince. He'd be spending an inordinate amount of time practicing with Cadence. I'd have to find some excuses to hang around. No one messed with my best friend. And Jordan looked like a guy on the prowl.

"So meet in my dorm or yours for dinner?"

I blinked as Cady's words brought me back to the present.

"Um, wherever is fine. Your mom going to sign us both out for the evening?" Mrs. Cole was on my list of approved people with the school. Our families had been close since before Cady and I had been friends.

"Yep. Gosh, I'm so excited, Zane. I can literally feel my adrenal glands working overtime right now." She giggled, giddy with excitement.

I snorted. "Maybe lay off the coffee for the rest of the day, yeah?"

She nodded. "Okay. Meet me in my dorm commons then. Mom and Dad should be here around five. Ooh, maybe we can browse the mall after. I still have some Christmas shopping to get in, and there is going to be zero time for that now. Seriously. Tonight is probably the last time I'll leave campus between now and show night."

"You're not wrong. You'll be dreaming pirouettes and jazz hands from now until Christmas." I chuckled at her manically excited expression.

CADENCE

Sure enough, James Alderton, world-famous choreographer, arrived right on time the next week, and by one o'clock, I was feeling the burn.

"No, no, no!" Mr. Alderton shouted at me for the third time in a row. Heat blasted across my cheeks as he corrected me again. "You put your feet like this. If you don't, you won't be able to execute the next twist cleanly. Do it again."

I was a champ at picking up new choreography. I memorized instantly, my muscles automatically knowing how to move and what to do. That happened when you'd been dancing since you were practically in diapers.

But not this time. This was a sequence of moves like I'd never seen. *Nutcracker, The Alternate* was a ballet comprised of a combination of different dance styles. It was brilliant—this was something brand new in the dance world—*and I was going to be a part of it*—if I could get my brain and normally coordinated limbs to call off their impasse.

It did not bode well.

"Jordan, we're going through the whole thing. You'll do the lift and twist. Your teacher will spot behind you."

Nerves writhed in my gut.

Mr. Alderton cued the music, and it was time to run it again.

I hit every note, my feet in the correct position until the final twist. I didn't get good lift, and consequently, Jordan struggled to heft my slight frame to the full height. His hands gripped me, one on my hip, one braced against my belly. I teetered, using every muscle in my abdomen to remain still and with my limbs held rigid like I was supposed to.

It was no use.

With a curse, Jordan wavered, and then I was falling. Hard.

The spotter should have caught me fully, but as it was, he only managed to break my fall. With a few internal curses of my own, I landed gracelessly in a heap on the lightly padded mat.

Jordan ran frustrated hands through his sweat–dampened hair, glowering. I wanted to wither on the spot.

"Ms. Greystoke, I thought you said these were the best your school had to offer?" Mr. Alderton railed, flapping his arms akimbo.

Ms. Greystoke remained impassive. "This is an unusual sequence, unique to the Alderton style. They will learn it. This is the first day." She speared Jordan and me with a look.

My excitement of the first morning of rehearsals was ash in my gut. Determination still flared hot in my chest. I would do this. *I had to.* My desired future likely depended on a clean execution.

"We'll pick up in the morning. See that you work on your own time." Mr. Alderton flipped his fingers like he washed his hands of the lot of us, then stalked through the door.

Ms. Greystoke faced us. "You have lots of work to do. You can do this, but make no mistake, this will take over every minute of your lives from now until the final curtain call."

"Sorry about that," Jordan said as we ambled toward the door.

"Me, too. I'll work on getting those steps right."

"You will. We'll be stunning together." He smiled, his blond hair damp and clinging to his head. His hand brushed over my elbow.

I smiled. "We will."

"Hey, do you want to grab dinner and go through things again after? I've got homework I have to get done, and my arms need a break first," Jordan asked me as Ms. Greystoke exited through the door, along with most of the other students who had been in rehearsal.

"I can practice after dinner. We need to. But I'm having dinner at the café on campus with Channi. It's our thing." I gulped water from my red water bottle and screwed the cap back on. It was our weekly girls' night. We got meal passes to use in the café instead of the cafeteria and had girl time.

"Oh, dinner with Channi?"

My head jerked up. Jordan had a tone when he said Channi's name. I took another swig from my bottle and studied him. Was he *interested* in my best friend? I hid the smile trying to curl the corner of my mouth.

"I'll talk to her. I'll text you if she says it's okay for you to come." I grinned at him.

He raised an eyebrow as his lips curved.

"Sounds good."

"Channi," I squeaked as soon as she walked in the door, duffle slung over her shoulder. She dropped it to the floor with a thud.

"What?"

"Jordan wants to have dinner with us. I think with *you.*"

Channi's mouth dropped into an O. "Jordan Hazlet? Hot Jordan? Jordan with biceps the size of my thighs and a chest more sculpted than a marble statue? *That* Jordan?"

"That Jordan. The very same Jordan I know you've been ogling on the sly for months. He asked about dinner and then practicing. But he sounded particularly interested once I mentioned tonight was dinner with *you.*"

"Wow. I mean, are you sure he wasn't asking you to dinner?"

I shook my head, freshly washed hair swishing down my back. "Nope. I think his interests lie with a certain Sugar Plum Fairy."

Channi cupped her cheeks, her dark eyes sparkling in excitement.

"Should I tell him it's a yes then?"

She nodded. Emphatically. "But maybe we should call Zane to see if he can show up, too. Like, it's weird just the three of us, you know?"

"I'll text Jordan and call Zane right now." I grinned so hard my lips hurt. I so wanted Channi to find a guy. She deserved someone awesome. On those same lines, I wouldn't mind a guy myself, though any thoughts of dating were off the table for the next two weeks until the big performance was over.

"We're having dinner on girls' night?" Zane's confused voice filtered over the phone.

I laughed. "Yes. Unless you're doing dude night or something. Jordan is coming, and Channi and I want you there for moral support."

"Wait, moral support? Jordan? Who is Jordan coming to dinner with? Why are we doing this?"

I rolled my eyes as I wedged the phone between my chin and shoulder and put a fresh layer of deodorant on. I'd showered once but knew I'd be sweating again if we were practicing after dinner. "Jordan and I have to practice tonight. I'm not getting the steps, and if I'm honest, his lifting leaves a little to be desired. I'm already bruised. But we decided to have dinner, and he got all excited when I mentioned tonight was girls' night with Channi, so we all decided to go together. We need you so I don't have to sit by myself and watch them make googly eyes at each other."

There was a long pause on the other end. Channi turned the shower off in the bathroom and I knew she'd be out soon.

"Zane?"

"Are you sure he wants to go to dinner with Channi?"

"Zane!" I reprimanded. "Why would you say that? Of course, he does."

"I didn't mean it like that. I mean, I've seen him...watching you."

"I'm her best friend. I'm always with her."

"That is true." He sighed. "Alright. Dinner. Café, or somewhere else?"

"Café. We're just expanding girls' night to include the two of you. Don't you feel special?"

"I bow under the weight of the honor bestowed upon me."

I snorted. "See you in fifteen."

"Yeah." His tone was not enthusiastic.

ZANE

I got to the café ahead of everyone else and stood leaning against the doorjamb, waiting for Jordan and the girls. It's possible I also stewed a little. I didn't think Jordan was after Channi. I'd specifically seen him watching Cady that afternoon when I'd dropped by their practice to watch. I showed up to a lot of Cady's practices—it was almost more habit that anything. Something I'd done for years since my brother Austin and Cady had often been in the same classes. Even if Jordan hadn't been staring at Cady, I wasn't sure he was good enough for either of my friends.

Jordan was an excellent dancer. Austin only barely beat him out last year for the lead role in the winter production. Austin was a year ahead of Jordan, and by all accounts, the more experienced dancer. But Jordan had that natural athlete's grace. It had been close. I could not fault him there. But as a guy? I wasn't sure how he leveled up.

Zane is still having an Emotional reaction to what is going on with Cady. This also shows a level of inner Vulnerability where she is concerned. These things can be apparent to the reader, even if they're not always clear yet to the character.

"Hey Zane, what are you doing down here?" Amy Trent asked as she sauntered in, freshly showered, her hair still wet.

"Waiting for Cady and Channi."

"We should hang out sometime." Her eyes slit almost predatorily.

"You take a sudden interest in guitar? Maybe the sound-board?" I asked, not working too hard at hiding my sar-casm.

"Haha, funny, Zane. No. We've been going to this school for four years together. We've had classes together. But we've never hung out. We should." She smiled prettily, verging on coy.

I spied Cady and Channi walking through the doors on the opposite side of the room and internally sighed in relief.

"Yeah, there's probably a reason for that," I quipped, nodded, then left. I steeled myself for another awkward conversation as Jordan trailed in after the girls.

Once we had our meals, we settled at a table in the far corner. I slid into the booth next to Cady, letting Channi share her space with Jordan. Cady's leg pressed against mine, and I was strangely aware of it. Probably because I was on high alert with Jordan potentially on the prowl.

Zane has a <u>Reaction</u> to the <u>Physical Action</u> of Cady's leg pressed against his.
Even though there is nothing romantic meant in Cady's proximity, Zane still feels these actions.

CADENCE

"So what do you guys think about James Alderton? I mean, how epic is it that we are actually performing one of his pieces under his direct supervision?" Channi gushed as she speared a piece of steamed broccoli off her plate.

"I heard that he and Ms. Greystoke knew each other in college. I bet that's the only reason Archibald got Alderton here. Not that Archibald isn't deserving—we are the premier boarding dance academy in the country, but isn't this the first time Alderton has stepped down from the world circuit to do something on such a small scale?" Jordan asked.

"If he and Ms. Greystoke have history, that would make sense," I offered, carefully watching Jordan for any signs of attraction toward Channi so I could report back, and we could overanalyze the entire meal back in our dorm room later. "Whatever the reason, I'm certainly glad he's here and we're doing *Nutcracker, The Alternate*. This puts Archibald—and us by extension—on the dance map like nothing else could at this point in our careers." I still got a little giddy thinking about it.

"I bet they knew each other way back. For Alderton, Archibald is like a snack," Channi said.

Jordan snorted. "That rhymed."

Channi giggled as a girlish flush stole over her cheeks. "I guess it did."

Zane rolled his eyes good naturedly. "Poet and didn't know it."

I poked him in the ribs, and he flinched. "Woman, don't be cruel."

"He'll have to challenge you to a duel," Jordan quipped.

"Don't be a fool," Channi said with a goofy smile, eyes twinkling.

The conversation quickly devolved from there, each of us trying to make up a rhyme more outrageous than the one before us. All considered, it was a pleasant forty-five minutes of dinner, but we still had work to do.

"Ready to try that lift again?" Jordan asked as we put the last of our trash into the bins.

"Needs must," I replied, thinking of the already-discolored patches on my hips from that afternoon's practice.

"It was nice having dinner," Channi offered.

"Yeah, thanks for letting me barge in on girls' night. It was *cool*," Jordan ended on one more rhyming word and winked at her. Definitely a good sign.

I was favoring my sore ribs and hips, struggling into my sweatshirt the next morning, as my bare foot landed on a square of paper near the door.

Looking down, I blinked, a grin curving the corner of my mouth.

"Channi, I think Jordan left you a note!" I squealed as I snatched the envelope that had been slid under the door. "Look!" There was no name on the outside of the envelope, just a quick flourish and a *C*.

"For me?"

"I think it has to be. Who would be sending me notes? Besides, doesn't this look like a *C*? Let's open it." I wiggled my eyebrows at her.

Channi nodded and I tore into the envelope like a three-year-old. I unfolded the paper and read:

Dancing is all we do

Let's do something else, too

After Christmas, let's go on a date

Once we're done with Nutcracker, The Alternate

"Well, it has to be to you. It's written in verse! You're the one who started that last night." I skimmed the short missive again. "His rhyming prowess isn't the most impressive thing I've ever read, but cheese and crackers, Jordan wants to date you!" I whisper-shrieked, so as not to alert the rest of the dorm.

Channi stood in the middle of the room, her eyes wide, mouth dropped open.

"This is one of the coolest things *ever*." She glanced up at me. "I mean, who writes poetry to woo a girl anymore? Men should revive this custom!"

I snorted, unable to help myself. "But maybe do it a bit better than Jordan." We giggled and Channi reverently refolded the note and put it on her dresser.

"Why am I so nervous? What am I going to say if I see him today at practice?" Channi fiddled with the end of her sleek black braid.

"I know. Let's have a study session tonight. At practice, I'll tell Jordan to meet us in the library after dinner. I'll make an excuse and make a getaway and leave the two of you to plot your date."

Channi bit her lip. "Let's do it."

ZANE

I turned in my test—the last test of the semester—for senior-level physiology and heaved a sigh of relief. It was the last major requirement I had for this semester. I could put all my attention on my music and running the sound board for the ballet.

There weren't many of us who wanted to focus on musical production; most of the music students at Archibald wanted to be world-famous dancers. It was a lucky break for me, because it was me and James who were in charge of the sound board for the production, and we didn't have to share the spotlight. There were other students doing the behind-the-scenes things, but it would be just the two of us mixing the boards.

"Zane, wait up."

I paused, resisting the urge to roll my eyes as Amy Trent rushed up, her large eyes sparkling with some shimmery powder on her lids.

"Hey, Amy," I said conversationally.

"I'm free for lunch. You should come eat with me." She literally batted her eyelashes. Did that ever work?

"Sorry. Meeting James to talk soundboard stuff."

She pouted. "You don't like me very much, do you?"

Not especially. "I hardly know you well enough to dislike you."

"Then why won't you come have lunch with me? You could *get* to know me."

She put her hand on my arm, squeezing to stop me. I turned to face her. "Why the sudden interest?"

Amy shrugged and smiled. "Maybe I've noticed you." She licked her bottom lip.

Actually licked her bottom lip while staring at me from under her lashes.

"That's nice."

"Ah, Zane, don't play hard to get." She ran her hand a few inches up my arm and I forced my lip not to curl.

Note how Amy's touch, as opposed to Cady's touch, has the opposite effect on Zane. It highlights the Reaction Zane has to Cady's Physical Actions.

"Amy, I'm flattered. But I really don't see a future here." I was baffled at her sudden attention. If it had been any other girl, I probably would have been a lot more interested. But Amy Trent had set my teeth on edge the first time I saw her—she'd been berating another student for taking the seat she wanted in the science classroom.

"Give me a chance to change your mind."

I sighed. She was like a dog with a bone.

"What's your favorite cookie?" she cajoled.

"I like chocolate chip."

"You like chocolate chip, or that's just what Cadence likes, and you feel like you have to agree? Is *she* why you won't go out with me?" She pouted.

"What? No, Cady likes sugar cookies." Heat built in my stomach, some foreign emotion curling in my stomach at the thought of swearing off other girls because of Cady.

"You really should look at someone who can at least get their dance steps right," Amy said, anger darkening her features.

Indignation simmered under my skin, and I reeled the don't-you-dare-talk-about-my-best-friend-beast back in. "Yep. This is why we aren't ever going out."

Shaking my head, I turned and walked down the hall, ready to leave Amy and the rigors of school behind until next semester, but Amy's words nagged at me—not just the mean ones—as I headed to my dorm.

Cady wasn't the reason I never really dated. I just hadn't met a girl I wanted to date that badly yet. That was all.

Wasn't it?

Zane is having strong
Emotion regarding Cady.

Even if he is still oblivious.

CADENCE

Practice felt especially brutal that afternoon. Our classes had lightened up with the coming of performance night, so I was taking advantage of the mental break and pushing my body to its limits, trying to get this last sequence down.

It didn't matter what we did—Jordan and I could not get ourselves synced right to do the final lift.

"I'm calling it," Mr. Alderton said nearly an hour after practice should have ended. "The two of you are just going to have to work on these steps more. We'll address it again tomorrow. After that you need a day off to rest and recuperate before dress rehearsal and the performance. So help me if the audience leaves because the leads can't get the steps right," he muttered as he left the room.

My cheeks burned and a sick feeling rooted in the pit of my stomach as I took my slippers off and the rest of the dancers cleared the room until it was just me and Jordan left with our failure.

Jordan wiped a towel over his face. "I need you to really work on keeping yourself straight. I can't hold you steady if your body is bending," he said as he squirted water into his mouth.

Anger flared beneath my skin. "I can't keep myself steady if you don't get your hands in the right place. You twist your palms and I go sideways." I deflated. "I need to work on the launching, too. You'd be able to catch me easier if I got better height on the leap."

"That's true. We'll get it, though; don't worry." He smiled tiredly. "So, did you—"

"Actually," I interrupted him, "Channi and I are study-ing in the library after dinner. Want to come?"

A grin cracked his face. "Sure. That'd be great."

"Cool. I'll see you there."

"Definitely. Hey, did you—"

"Hey, Cady. Jordan," Zane said as he walked through the doors.

"Zane? What are you doing here?" I asked, turning from Jordan to face Zane.

"Sorry, am I interrupting?" Zane said, looking from me to Jordan, an unreadable expression on his face.

"Oh, no. We're done. See you tonight?" I waved to Jordan and grabbed my bag.

"Sure. Sounds good," Jordan said tightly.

Zane tipped his head at Jordan and walked me out of the practice room.

"What's up?"

ZANE

I'd made a habit of being in the vicinity when Cady and Jordan practiced after hours. Because some part of me was nervous about the two of them being alone together. My gut clenched. I didn't want to explore that too closely.

I swallowed. "Well, I wanted to catch you before you heard this from anyone else."

Cady's eyes got big, and her eyebrows hiked up her forehead.

"Amy has been hitting on me."

Cady's mouth dropped open. "Oh, Zane, please tell me you're not going out with her. I get that you're all grown up and allowed to have a girlfriend, but please don't let it be her. She's completely reprehensible."

"Would you let me finish?" I admonished gently.

"Sure. Sorry."

"She's been hitting on me," I repeated. The icy wind blasted me in the face as I held the door open for Cady. "But I think she's doing it as a way to try to undermine you. Ashton asked me if I was dating Amy, then told me she's been making snide remarks about you and the dance steps. Trying to usurp your part. I know how hard you've worked for this. You *deserve* this part. Don't let her words get to you. I wouldn't have said anything at all, but I didn't want you to hear it in passing and think I was hiding something like this. I'm definitely not." I stopped us with a hand on her elbow. "You okay?"

She took a big breath, white pluming in front of her face as she blew it out. "I'm processing. And I'm angry. Angry at her, and angry with myself. The steps are killer. Jordan and I just can't seem to find that happy place where we lift well. Either his hands are in the wrong place, I get my feet tangled, or my launch isn't high enough." Defeat sounded in her voice as she shivered.

"Come on. You're sweaty. You need to get out of the cold." I turned us, letting my hand linger a moment longer on her back. "Stop worrying so much. You're going to nail this."

Zane consciously lets his hand linger. He is beginning to have awareness of his <u>Attraction</u>.

"I wish I had your confidence." She sniffed.

"Cady, are you crying?" My protective best friend hackles immediately raised and went on high alert.

"No. Not really. I probably need to have a good cry and get it all out before performance night."

I nodded. That was Cady's habit. How she coped. I hated that I'd brought her news that had tipped her emotional scales, but still, better out before performance night than on it.

Cady sniffled again. "Thanks for letting me know, Zane. I've got a study session in the library tonight."

"With Jordan?"

"And Channi. Catch you tomorrow on our run?"

"I'll be there." I smiled at her, and she returned it, kindling something warm in my gut. It mixed with a hint of loss—I suddenly wished I was going to be studying at the library tonight.

Zane is feeling <u>Emotion</u> and having a <u>Reaction</u> to it.

Jealousy is a powerful motivator.

CADENCE

The library was warm and cozy, lit with soft orange lights as the scent of old books lingered in the air. It was a nice change from sweat and musty gym mats. I made sure I was intentionally late, and a smile curved my lips as I saw Channi and Jordan already seated at a table, books open between them. Firing off a quick text to Zane to have him call me in twenty minutes, I stopped and watched them a second. Jordan looked bored as Channi pointed to something in his book with her pencil. Her fat black braid fell over her shoulder as she glanced back down at her notebook.

Jordan cracked his neck and caught sight of me lingering near the shelves. I smiled brightly and walked over to them.

"Hi, guys. Sorry I'm late. Lost track of time." I snatched a look at their open books. "Ah. The calc quiz tomorrow?"

"You know it," Channi said with a tight smile. I resisted the urge to let my brows meet, wondering at the cause of her pinched expression.

"Calc is my favorite," Jordan added sarcastically.

"Yeah, mine, too," I muttered as I dug out my own notebook with notes. Not that I had any intention of sticking around very long. Blessedly, math came easily to me, and I had studied over lunch. I was prepared.

For the calc quiz, anyway.

Nutcracker; The Alternate, not so much.

"Sorry, I didn't mean to interrupt—go ahead with whatever you were explaining, Channi," I encouraged.

"Hang on," Jordan said, glancing at my pristine notes. "This right here." He pointed to a line in the example problem. "Can you explain how this part works?" he asked me, making eye contact as he raised his head.

"Oh. Sure." I frowned on the inside, wishing he'd let Channi explain, but figured I should keep up the charade, and launched into an explanation.

My phone buzzed and flashed Zane's name across the screen thirteen minutes later. He always was punctual.

"Sorry. Gotta take this." I grabbed my phone and answered in a whisper so I wouldn't get in trouble if any librarian happened to be watching.

"Hey," I answered.

"Hi. Why am I calling you? Aren't you having a study session?" Zane asked on the other line.

"Are you serious?" I made sure my tone matched my words.

"Um, yes?"

"No, of course I'll come." I sounded urgent.

"Am I meeting you somewhere?" Zane asked, amusement now evident in his voice.

"Sure. Just give me a few minutes to get there. Yeah. No. Be careful. I'll be right there."

Zane snorted. "I expect a full report. I'm in my dorm commons."

"Okay. Bye."

"Bye." Zane hung up, but I could practically hear him smiling through the phone line.

I turned back to Jordan and Channi. "Guys, I'm so sorry. Zane is having a family crisis. I have to run. Sorry!" I hastily grabbed my books, shoved them in my bag, and made a beeline for the door.

The wind was brisk, and I was shivering by the time I made it through the light dusting of snow fluttering down to Zane's dorm. It was still during open commons, so I walked on in.

The commons room was empty, save Zane perched on a couch, his guitar balanced in his lap. He glanced up and grinned at me, one eyebrow raised higher than the other.

"I take it I had some sort of emergency?" he said mockingly as he put his guitar down, propping it against the arm of the couch.

"You did. Thanks for being a good sport."

"Well, tell me all about it so I'm in on the cover story." He patted the seat next to him and I plopped my bag and my body down beside him. Unwinding my scarf, I met his green gaze.

"I needed an excuse to leave Channi and Jordan studying alone in the library."

Zane shook his head and rolled his eyes. "I hope that doesn't come back to bite you in the butt."

"Why would it?" I frowned at him as I shrugged out of my coat.

"Have you really thought about the two of them together? I don't think they make a good match."

I stuck my tongue out at him.

"And I still maintain Jordan is into *you*, not Channi."

I opened my mouth to argue.

"And before you lay into me, it's not because I don't think Channi is a great girl."

I pursed my lips shut and glared at him for good measure. He arched a brow and my expression fell. "Fine," I conceded. "But she likes him, so at least try to be supportive."

He grunted.

I sighed and slouched back against the couch, my leg touching Zane's. We were quiet a minute. Zane picked his guitar back up and strummed softly, not singing, though I loved it when he did. His voice was rich and mellow, quiet, but full of strength and soul.

"What's eating at you, Cady? You're moping."

"Am I?"

"Mm-hmm," he rumbled. Skitters of something tickled over my arms at the sound.

"It's the ballet," I said at length, fretting my lower lip with my teeth. "I can't get my steps right. They don't feel like natural movements in my ballet shoes. I have never struggled this much learning choreography in my entire life. I know what to do, but my body refuses to cooperate. I'm starting to panic. I've got days to get this perfect. The rest of my career may depend on it." Tears burned the back of my eyes at the admission. But Zane was safe. I could tell him. He wouldn't judge or ridicule me.

Zane squeezed my knee. "I think you're getting inside your head. Run through the steps. I'll watch your feet for you," Zane offered, putting his guitar aside.

"Yeah?"

"Of course." He smiled at me, his eyes intense and his grin crooked on the one side. My heart fluttered at the unwavering support I found there.

I blew out a breath. "Okay." I hauled myself off the couch and tied my slippers back on. "Count me off," I said.

"Gotta make sure you have the right cadence." He cracked another lopsided grin.

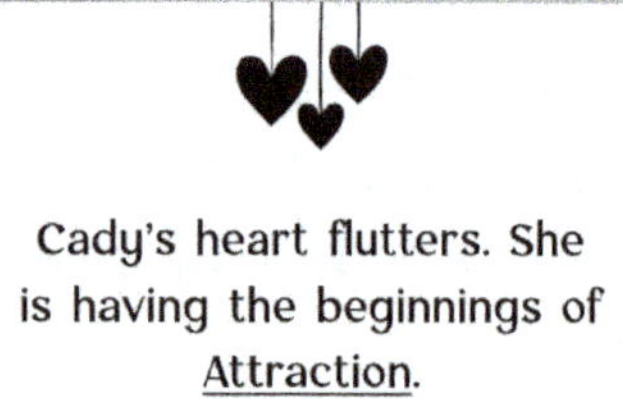

Cady's heart flutters. She is having the beginnings of <u>Attraction</u>.

"Haha," I muttered, rolling my eyes at his attempt to joke about my name.

"No, I'm serious. You're stuck in your head, and you're not feeling the music. Give it a go. Feel the cadence. Feel the beat. Move your body with it, not just the mechanics of the steps."

I sighed but nodded. He was right. He'd grown up with ballet nearly as much as I had, considering Austin's involvement, and I knew Zane had an accurate point about my headspace, mechanics, and the music. I paced to the other side of the commons so I'd have plenty of room and Zane could analyze my feet. He snapped his fingers, giving me the beat of the opening music. Gracefully swinging my arms out to my sides, my heart was strangely calm—no anxiety doing these movements with my best friend.

As the imaginary music sounded in my brain in time to Zane's snapping, I began the sequence of complicated movements. In, out, over, twist, leg up, arms sweep, twist again and turn, and CLANG! Someone dropped something heavy on the floor above us.

Adrenaline surged at the unexpected noise, my feet tangled, ankles bent, and arms flailed as I crashed onto the couch and face planted into Zane's chest.

"Gotcha!"

I practically head-butted Zane, flinging him back against the couch with a grunt. His hands closed around my waist, and heat surged through me. My insides quivered with...something I'd never felt for Zane before. Raising my head, I met his gaze.

Green eyes stared back at me, wide, surprised, and intense. Suddenly my mouth was dry, and my pulse picked up. Something sparked between us, though I didn't have the right words to describe it.

His fingers tightened around my middle. His Adam's apple bobbed slightly as his eyes searched my face. My lips parted, unsure what this unspoken thing between us was, but finding it exhilarating and terrifying all at once.

For one moment, we were suspended in a bubble of our own making. Me, pressed against his chest, his hands splayed wide, holding me fast.

"So help me, that better not be fornication I'm hearing out here!" A door slammed open and Bobby Duke, Zane's RD, stepped out of his quarters just off the common room. "Oh, it's you two. Whew." He literally wiped a hand across his forehead as my cheeks flamed and Zane squirmed slightly. "You wouldn't believe what I've caught kids trying to do out here." He leaned casually against the wall of the hallway as Zane and I struggled to break away.

"Sorry, I—I tripped. This new footwork is horrendous," I stammered, backing away from the couch a few steps.

Bobby chuckled. "Greystoke has been talking about all the progress in the teacher's lounge.

I'm looking forward to seeing the final production."

Snakes writhed in my gut as I thought about the final performance mere days away.

"I hope I don't fall on my face for it," I mumbled, cheeks still hot. I fidgeted, nervous and unsure of myself. Zane sat, a slightly confused expression on his face.

"Nonsense. You'll be fine, kid," Bobby said, shoving his hands in his pockets. "Let's see it again. No tripping this time."

"Oh, um," I stammered.

"Pshaw. None of that. Here. All Jordan does is a catch, lift, and a twirl you, doesn't he? Here. Let's practice. I'll be Jordan." He pushed away from the wall.

Bobby was nice and all but...

"I'll do it. You watch and tell us what needs to change," Zane said quickly, practically leaping from the couch. He quirked an eyebrow at me as relief flooded my system.

Bobby snorted. "Zane, have you ever done a catch, lift, and twirl in your life? I mean, we all know you're a musical genius. But dancing isn't your forte." Bobby's eyebrows scrunched.

Zane shrugged. "I did ballet when I was younger, and I've practiced plenty, both with Cadence and with Austin. No sweat. It's not like I'm trying to lift a three-hundred-pound gorilla." He winked at me, and for no good reason, my insides sparkled erratically.

"It's the tights. That's why Zane refuses to dance," I teased him. Zane chuckled, shrugging again and cocking an eyebrow mischievously.

"Some guys just aren't secure enough in their manhood."

"Ew, Bobby, please stop there," I begged.

"There is nothing wrong with my manhood," Zane muttered darkly with an eye roll.

Bobby sighed dramatically. "Fine. All right. Twirl it, girl." He motioned circles with his finger and planted himself where he could analyze my every move. Bobby had graduated from Archibald last year, was doing some advanced choreography workshops and teaching part time on campus, and was a little bit of a weirdo, but he did know dance. And right now, I could use all the help I could get.

"And go," Bobby said.

Zane counted off instead of snapping. Hearing the beat and listening for the music in my head, I took a breath, centering myself, then looked at Zane. He was ready, arms extended slightly. I went through the sequence.

In, out, over, twist, leg up, arms sweep, twist again and turn, skip and a leaping jump!

Zane's wide hands gripped my hips, and my feet never touched the ground. For five seconds I was flying as he gently spun me. We lurched slightly to the side and my eyes widened as I squeaked.

"Sorry. I've got you," Zane said, crushing me to his chest instead of lightly turning me down to land. "I'm a little out of practice," he said sheepishly as his hands found my upper arms and Bobby snorted.

"Again," Bobby said. "That wasn't bad, Cadence. Have confidence in your movements. You hesitate before the final lunge. Zane, compensate to the right side if she hesitates again. I won't have broken ankles in my dorm."

"Hey," Zane said quietly, gently pressing his fingers against my upper arms. "You know I'd never let you fall, right?"

"I know that," I replied, finding his gaze focused on mine, his dark fringe of lashes making my stomach curl pleasantly.

Emotion and Vulnerability are displayed with Zane's words, and Cady Reacts both Emotionally and Physically.

He nodded. "Good. Then don't hesitate. I'll catch you." He smiled, green eyes twinkling as the slight dimple on his left cheek appeared.

"You'd better catch me," I mumbled with a raised eyebrow before heading to the other end of the room again.

"I'll catch you," Zane repeated as I turned to face him.

"Don't worry about that part. He might not be Jordan with biceps of steel, but you weigh as much as a twig. You'll be peachy. I've seen Zane lift in the weight room with his brother. He'll catch you just fine, even if his finesse needs some work." Bobby offered his encouragement. I resisted the urge to roll my eyes.

But he did have one thing right.

I knew Zane would catch me.

This was it. No hesitation.

In, out, over, twist, leg up, arms sweep, twist again and turn, skip and leap!

"Up you go," Zane said as his hands connected to my hips, gripping and hoisting me up over his head, turning slowly, making a much more graceful landing this time.

"Much better! Again," Drill Sergeant Bobby commanded.

"Caught you," Zane teased, squeezing my hip once before releasing me.

Ooh. Glittery tingles danced inside me. I never reacted to pressure on my hips like that when Jordan held them for that part of the dance. I filed that away to never think about again.

"Come on. Snap, snap," Bobby said, snapping his fingers. "That was much better. You didn't hesitate. You felt the movement. Do it again. Anticipate the movement this time."

Zane squeezes her hips, a <u>Physical Action</u>, and Cady <u>Reacts</u> with <u>Attraction</u>.

I tried again. And again.

For the next half hour, we practiced until Zane complained.

"Okay. I think I need to call it quits. My arms are limp spaghetti noodles. I told you I'd catch you; I need to stop to keep my promise. I don't want the retribution if I accidentally drop you."

I snorted, verging on exhaustion myself.

"Yeah, all right. I guess you can stop." Bobby's phone rang. He dug it out of his pants pocket and swiped the screen. "Oh, crap. I was supposed to call my girlfriend an hour ago. I'm in for it now. Have a good night, kids," Bobby said with a dismissive wave as he trudged back into his apartment.

Part of me wanted to stick my tongue out at him for assuming he was my boss, but I was just too tired.

Zane leaned back and stretched his back with a grimace. "Feel better about the steps at least?" he asked.

I sighed and bent to grab my scarf. "I do. It...I don't know. It's so much easier to do it with you instead of Jordan. It shouldn't be this hard. Like, I know I'm complicating it in my head, but I feel like there's some mental block. It's probably the stress of thinking about scouts and everyone else watching me do this move I'm not one-hundred percent confident about on stage. All the spotlights."

He waited as I shrugged back into my coat.

"Come on, I'll walk you back to your dorm." He shoved his arms through the sleeves of his hoodie he'd abandoned on the couch. "Oh. Yep, I'm gonna hurt tomorrow," he groaned.

I smiled. "I *do* appreciate the sacrifice."

"Yeah, I know." Zane smiled back. "Also, stay out of your head. You can do this. You just proved you can. My arms will never work right again, but we know you *can* do this sequence."

"*Can* is an awfully big word sometimes."

ZANE

Oh man. Oh man, oh man, oh man. Cady had boobs. And hips. And curves. I couldn't ignore them when they'd been pressed up against me and I'd been holding her up in the air, hands on her hips, eyes trying not to trace her chest.

Curves. My best friend. She had them. And I was *unbelievably* aware of them now. How had I not realized she was all...girly? And why did I care?

That was a stupid question.

I cared for the same reason I wanted to murder Jordan every time I caught him looking at Cady.

I was jealous.

Fire raced under my skin. My breath hitched in my lungs as I stood there like an idiot in the chilly wind outside her dorm, even after she'd gone in.

Shaking my head, I trudged back toward my dorm, hands shoved in my pockets, brain processing, emotions in a tangle. Memories of Cadence rammed through my brain. Her kindness, her courage, her determination, her silly grins. I don't know how I never realized it...but now that I'd acknowledged it, I couldn't make it go away.

It wasn't just her newly discovered curves. They were just the spark that lit the powder keg.

I loved Cady.

As more than my best friend.

Something happened in those thirty charged seconds when she fell against my chest before Bobby totally ruined the moment. But even so, it was probably good he had. I'd nearly lost my mind and kissed her. What would have become of our friendship then?

Amy was right. Cady *was* why I'd never looked at other girls.

Oh, this was awkward.

Sadness engulfed me as I realized in what a lonely position I now found myself. I couldn't very well blurt my newfound feelings out, or I'd risk losing the most important relationship of my life. If I kept them bottled inside, I might die of bitterness.

Patience. I needed patience. I blew a hot breath out and ran a hand through my hair. For sure I couldn't do anything about anything until after Christmas. Cady needed all her focus on her performance. She needed me to be chill, support her, and not rip Jordan's arms off.

I hoped I could do that last one.

> Zane has strong physical **Attraction** to Cady. It encompasses his **Emotions** and a layer of **Vulnerability** because she is also his best friend.

CADENCE

I took my time walking up the stairs to my dorm room after I left Zane at the door. I slowed even more as I reached the sitting area on the second floor. It was empty, and I glided to the window that overlooked the wooded area of campus. Night had fallen, and stars twinkled down onto the fresh dusting of snow.

My brain replayed the last hour over and over.

Zane.

Zane.

Zane.

His name crescendoed in my head with every beat of my treacherous heart.

I swallowed. Whatever had happened between us tonight had altered the way I felt about my best friend. I shook my head but allowed myself to admit that I wanted *more* with Zane McAlister. I took a deep inhale through my nose and blew it out my mouth.

I wasn't sure how I should proceed with this.

With no answers forthcoming, I trudged down the hallway to my room.

"Hiya," Channi said from her bed as I shut the door.

"Hey," I said, surprised to see her. "I figured you'd still be studying with Jordan in the library. How'd it go after I left?" I shoved thoughts of Zane from my mind and tried to focus on my other best friend and her current love life.

Channi grimaced. "It lasted all of ten minutes after you left."

"What? Why?" I asked, horrified on Channi's behalf.

"Mom called me. Aunt Bina and Uncle Ishir just found out they are pregnant. The whole family called to wish them well. I got five minutes of notice before I had to hop on the family call. My mother never plans ahead for anything." Channi rolled her eyes dramatically. "But another baby cousin will be fun."

I smiled. "That's true. We'll see if we can't manufacture some other reason to get the two of you together."

Channi smirked. "I have no doubt you'll think of something."

ZANE

The last day of practice rolled around. I cracked my knuckles, working out the kinks in my fingers, ready to master the sound board like a pro.

"My mom says that'll give you arthritis," James commented dryly, cracking his own fingers.

"Guess we'll find out, huh?" I grinned at him. He shrugged.

I liked James. He was competent in what he did, and I wasn't stressed about my co-leader for the sound board. But I *was* still stressed about Jordan and Cady. I'd been reading Cady like a book for years, yet where Jordan was concerned, I felt lost and out of the loop. I knew Cady was trying to get Channi and Jordan to date, so I assumed that was all the more her interest in Jordan went, but it was that nagging thought that maybe she was doing it to somehow weasel into his good graces that kept my blood pressure from settling.

I shook my head.

"You all right, man?" James asked.

I blinked. "Yeah. Totally fine."

I would be. I just had to survive this performance, make sure Cady did the best job she could by keeping her out of her own head, and then find the perfect time and place to declare my life-altering feelings to her.

Because if I told her what I felt for her, it *would* be life altering, one way or the other. The thought made me queasy. So instead of dwelling on it right now, I shoved it away and focused my attention where it belonged.

Then Cady stepped on stage and all my concentration fled.

So much for that.

She was in full costume for dress rehearsal, and I couldn't help but appreciate the way her legs looked. Jordan let his eyes slide over her, lingering on her chest. My eyeballs bulged in their sockets. I had to get this jealousy thing under control.

Shoving down my unhelpful thoughts, I muscled my way through the rehearsal, still contemplating what I should, or should not, say to Cady.

If only I'd known how soon that chance would find me.

I was being a total sap and walking over a note and a rose for Cady, wishing her luck on tomorrow's performance. Because I wanted to see her, not just text her like I normally would have. The need to be extra—more than her best friend—to let her see potential in me as something other than that, had my nerves strung tight. Crushing on my best friend had clearly addled my brain. Nevertheless, there I was, freezing as I entered her dorm commons.

*—I'm here. Come down? I want to wish you luck before tomorrow—*I texted her as I shivered in the welcome heat of her dorm lobby.

—Be right there—

"Zane?"

I groaned internally as Amy and a gaggle of her friends traipsed down the east stairwell and into the commons. She glided over to me, touching my bicep when she got close enough.

"What are you doing here?" she purred.

"Waiting for—" I didn't get to finish my sentence as one of Amy's friends bumped into me—it had to be on purpose, because no ballerina at Archibald was that clumsy—and I dropped both card and flower just as someone opened the door. A gust a frigid air whipped into the room and blew the card to who knows where. I couldn't see where it landed.

Growling in frustration, I bent and picked up the flower.

"Zane, after all that talk about not being interested. You little tease." Amy winked, plucked the rose right out of my hand. The girls tittered as she raised up on tip toe and placed a kiss on my cheek, careful to lean in and brush the length of her body against me.

I was so shocked, my feet grew roots, and my muscles seized.

Amy smiled sweetly, squeezed my shoulder, glanced quickly over her shoulder, and then exited the building with my rose and her she-herd in tow.

A strangled noise echoed from the western stairwell where Amy had glanced, and my heart fell even as I turned.

Cadence stood here, hand to her mouth, eyes shining of betrayal.

CADENCE

I couldn't believe what my eyes had just seen. Zane McAlister handed Amy-my-nemesis Trent a rose. And she kissed him. *She kissed him.* And she'd made sure I'd seen her do it. Seen Zane *let* her kiss him.

Tears burned the back of my eyes, and I quickly gulped them down.

"Cady, it's not what it looks like," Zane started, arms splayed helplessly.

I shook my head. The most important performance of my life to date was tomorrow, and I needed a clear head. I'd landed the last sequence today, but only barely. I could not afford to let my concentration waver. I could not be thinking of Zane and Amy. The mere idea of it was radiating a deep ache in my chest.

Swallowing hard, I took a breath. "It doesn't matter," I lied straight to his face. "I—you can date whoever you want. You don't need my permission." My voice cracked. "I can't deal with this right now though. I have to focus on tomorrow. Maybe...maybe we can talk after the show. Night, Zane." And I fled like a coward back up the stairs.

I went straight to the shower once I hit my room. I turned the water on as hot as I could stand and let my tears fall. I cried until I had no tears left, purging all the emotion from my system that I could. When I shut the water off, I felt as wrung out as the washcloth I slung over the edge of the shower rod.

I splashed cold water on my face, hoping it would tone down any residual redness. Of course, Channi noticed as soon as I exited the bathroom with a billow of steam.

"You okay? Are you super nervous about tomorrow?"

I was, so I wasn't lying when I nodded.

"You want a cup of tea?"

"Yeah," I rasped. "And I think I need a girl chat."

"Oh! Not just about tomorrow, then?"

I shook my head miserably as the whole sordid story came tumbling out.

Channi rubbed soothing circles on my back as we sipped our tea and I hiccuped.

"How long have you liked him like that? I had no idea. Obviously, he doesn't either."

"I don't even know. Consciously? Maybe a week? Unconsciously? Probably a lot longer. Because it's this intense sort of all-consuming sort of *like*."

Cady realizes the Vulnerability her Attraction to Zane holds for her. The situation complicates her Emotions and her Reaction.

"Why now?" Channi asked and took another gulp of her cranberry lemon tea.

"Probably because stupid Amy Trent wants him, and I realized he's not going to be off the market forever. He's never really dated, so I've never really had a chance to be jealous."

"Well, I don't profess to know much about love or dating, but I do know that Amy Trent is the southern end of a north-bound jackal and that you and Zane have been best friends for practically your whole lives. Friendships like that don't disappear overnight. They weather the ups and downs. I don't think you'll ever lose Zane. Even if he does like jackal-faced Amy Trent. But I still think it's unlikely that he does."

"Then why in the world would he let her kiss him?" I lamented, staring in the dregs of my spiced chai.

Channi shrugged. "I don't know. Maybe Amy is working an angle. I wouldn't put it past her."

"I suppose that's true."

Speculations aside, I still didn't sleep well.

It was one hour before the curtain rose. I'd purposefully called my parents this morning and then turned off my phone. I couldn't deal with the texts or calls I knew Zane would try to send. We didn't do conflict between us well, and part of me regretted not having it out with him the night before. The other part of me never wanted to talk about Zane and Amy in the same sentence ever.

My nerves were stretched taut as I limbered up my muscles. I wished I could stretch out my nerves the same way I could my calves. I eased my leg off the barre where I was working out the lingering tightness when Mina approached. Her flower fairy skirt swooshed, and her tap shoes hit an odd click as she walked.

"Hey Cadence. I found this on the floor on the way out of the dorm today. I didn't open it, so I don't know what it is, but it's got your name. Figured it fell off some flowers for you or something."

"Thanks, Mina." I took the green envelope, and my heart stuttered as I took in Zane's crooked but confident script. Mina found it on the floor of the dorm?

My heart rate doubled, and I swallowed as my fingers shook slightly, trying to open the card. He'd sketched a ballerina on the front. I touched my lips as they curved upward. Zane was a decent artist, and I was gratified that he'd gone to the trouble. Nerves ratcheted tight, I opened the card.

Cady,

Stay out of your head. You're going to kill it tomorrow. Do it just like you practiced. You won't fall. I know you can do it. I'll be cheering you from the sound booth.

-Z

Zane had brought me this...last night. Last night when I saw Amy kiss him. Had...had he been bringing *me* the flower and this card, and she happened to corner him? Heat slid through my chest. Folding the card and holding it close to my heart, I let myself inhale deeply a few times, centering myself and grounding my wild emotions. Zane was still my best friend. Amy hadn't thieved him away while I was busy trying set Channi up with Jordan. I still had a chance.

If I dared to take it.

I smiled as I tucked the card into my bag and finished stretching.

"You're looking super relaxed," Amy said as I took a drink from my water bottle, her eyebrow raised, something like a smile on her face.

"I guess so," I said, no longer feeling threatened by her. "I'm ready for this."

She pursed her lips before arranging her face into a smile. "I thought maybe we could bury the hatchet. Even though I'm the better dancer and should have had Marie's part, I'm determined not to be bitter about it. Here. I even made you some sugar cookies. Zane says they're your favorite." Amy looked like she had a fresh wedge of lemon stuck in her mouth as she tried for a grin, but I was too shocked to comment on it.

"Wow. Thanks. That's...really generous of you." I faltered for the right words.

She gave me a simpering smile and handed me a plate full of impressively iced cookies. "Break a leg!" Amy flounced away, her tutu of stiff sparkling tule bouncing haughtily over her rear end.

I snorted softly to myself. Strains of the orchestra finishing their warmup wafted backstage, and I glanced down at the sweet-laden plate in my hands. They looked delectable, and I likely would have eaten one right then merely for the quick energy, but all of them were iced in silky red frosting.

Which was a massive no-no when you had a Red-40 allergy.

"Oh man, are those cookies?" Carson asked as he sailed past, pausing as his eyes got huge in his face while his gaze raked over the treats.

I chuckled. "Yeah. Here. I can't eat them. Go ahead."

"Ah, man. Thanks! I need one of these about now."

I smiled as Carson grabbed a red-piped stocking-shaped cookie and popped half of it in his mouth as he continued on the way he was headed.

The performance was going off without a single hitch. Alderton could rest on his laurels if we finished as strong as we started. I was buzzing with nerves and energy as I came off stage having finished the last segment before my final scene, in which I did The Sequence, and the Nutcracker prince was revealed to the world.

With a solid fifteen minutes before I was needed back on stage, I swigged water and wandered to my designated spot, hoping to catch a glimpse of Channi through the curtain and calm the jitters still dancing powerfully through my midsection. All the agony would be over soon, one way or the other.

Just as Channi was twirling her last series of beautiful *pirouettes*, Jordan came up and stood behind me, his fingers ghosting over my elbow.

I sighed happily, forgetting my anxiety for a moment as I focused on my friend. "Channi danced perfectly. Isn't she beautiful out there?"

"Yeah, she's all right," Jordan said.

I glanced up at him sharply.

"What?" His blond eyebrows drew together.

"*All right?* That's it?"

He shrugged. "She's good. That's why she got the part. I mean, Amy could have done it just as well. You'd have done it better."

My mouth dropped open.

Jordan didn't seem to notice. "So, I've been wanting to ask you, but it's been hard to corner you alone—did you get my note?" Jordan turned and smiled at me, teeth showing.

I blinked. "Your note?" His note? What note had he sent me? The only note I'd received was Zane's.

"Yeah, the note. You know, asking if you wanted to go out after the performance."

"I never got that note." Jordan never sent me anything. What was he talking about?

"You didn't get the note? Man, I even wrote it in rhymes after we all ate at the café that night. I was hoping we could go out maybe tomorrow night." He gave me a smoldery grin and a clump of dread rose in my stomach.

"You, you left that note for Channi," I stammered. "Because you're interested in *her*. You put a *C* on the outside." *She's all right.* The lump of dread grew.

Jordan's smile fell. "Who? Channi? No, I'm not interested in her." He sneered. "Why would I want to date her? I left the note for *you*. *C* for *Cadence*. I want to go out with *you*."

"Oh, no." Anxiety multiplied and swarmed my insides.

"Oh, no, what?" Jordan's blond brows drew together again as his lips pursed.

I pinched the bridge of my nose. Why did he have to bring this up now? I was nervous enough as it was with the big sequence only minutes away. Now my whole body squirmed with guilt and regret. "I thought you were interested in Channi this whole time."

Jordan snorted. "Yeah. No. Not so much."

"But she likes you," I protested.

He shrugged. "She'll get over it. I'm not interested in her. What do you say though? We'd be a killer couple." He winked and my stomach dropped to my toes.

"Jordan, I'm sorry. I...I don't want to go out with you." Not when my heart beat only for my best friend with a flop of dark hair and emerald-green eyes.

Jordan's jaw clenched. "You're really stupid, you know that, Cadence?"

Anger bubbled inside me, mixing my emotions into a quagmire of explosive proportions. In that moment, I was so angry, I couldn't even speak.

"How could you be so stupid?" Jordan continued, his pride clearly affronted. "Of course, I wanted you. But forget it. I can't even look at you right now."

My heart plummeted as furious tears rimmed my eyes, and I thought I might be sick. Jordan stormed toward the door, missed a step, and went down with a sickening *crack*.

My hand flew to my mouth and Jordan's face paled ashy white.

"Jordan, what happened?" Ms. Greystoke, who had just entered the backstage area, flew to his side. His eyes rolled back in his head, and he fainted dead away. I was frozen in shock and abject horror.

Ms. Greystoke cursed before whipping out her phone. "You." She pointed to another student who had followed her. "Go get Alderton. Tell him we need Jordan's under-study. You—" She turned to me, her normally soft eyes hard and unyielding. "You will go out there and dance as if your life depends upon it. You will not think about Jordan. You will not let this distract you. You will go out and dance as the gifted young woman you are. Do you understand me?"

Hand still covering my mouth, and tears properly rimming my eyelids, I nodded, the horror of things fresh and unyielding. I swallowed down my emotions, determined to do my best despite the insane turn things had just taken.

Without feeling anything, I made my way to my spot behind the curtain. I couldn't even remember who Jordan's understudy was. I clutched my chest and willed the air to come in my nose and out my mouth. I felt like I was falling, pinwheeling, careening wildly and would crash to smithereens once I landed.

ZANE

Carson spewed his guts out not five feet from me.

"Dude," I nearly shouted. "What is wrong with you?" It came out sounding more accusatory than actually asking him what was wrong, even though I was genuinely concerned about him.

"I ate a cookie from the plate Amy gave Cadence. And Jordan just broke his foot. I've got to go dance." His cheeks puffed out again and I turned before I could watch him heave his guts into the trashcan again.

Fear stiffened my spine. Amy made Cady cookies? Ice trickled into my veins at the turn my thoughts took. If there was something wrong with the cookies that were intended for Cady...and..."What do you mean, *Jordan broke his foot?*"

"Just saw him getting loaded into an ambulance."

Carson was green. Cady might be sick. This was her big night. If she wasn't sick...I thought *I* might be sick at the next thought that rolled through my head.

"Go hydrate and sit down before you fall over. You can't dance like this."

"Have to," he heaved.

"You'll drop Cady before she's even in the air. You'll just hurt both of you. I'll take care of this." I turned to James, my co-sound operative. "You are in charge of the board. It had better be *perfect*." I would not allow anything to ruin Cady's night. James gulped and nodded as Carson sank to the floor, leaned against the wall of the booth.

I ran.

CADENCE

Panic set in hard as I took my place behind the curtain. Tears still wet my lashes and an enormous lump in my throat threatened to cut off my oxygen.

You can do this, I told myself. I had to. There was no other choice.

The music started and flower fairies tapped their metal shoes across the stage as a bead of sweat slipped between my shoulder blades.

"Why are you still dancing?" Amy ground out between her teeth as she came up behind me, dressed like Marie—like me. Chills whispered over my spine.

"Because this is *my* part," I answered, life springing back to my limbs at Amy's predatory expression.

"Didn't you eat the cookies I sent you?" she asked with a saccharine smile.

Unease slithered into my gut. "No, I didn't. I gave them to Carson," I finished slowly as disgust morphed into triumph on Amy's face.

"In that case, have fun. With Jordan out, Carson won't be far behind. There will be no Nutcracker prince. The only star in this show will be me."

"What do you mean Carson won't be far behind?"

Amy just smirked, turned her shoulder to me, and strutted away.

My eyes jerked back to the far side of the stage. Lalanna was nearly at the end of her ribbon routine and the tappers kept time in the background as she finished. If there was no understudy for the Nutcracker prince...

Just then, the bulbous head of the Nutcracker costume bobbled from the shadows to stand at his place opposite mine. He wiggled uncomfortably, yanking the front of his tunic down as far as it would go over the top of his tights, his hands fisting in frustration when the material refused to stretch any lower.

In a gesture I knew by heart.

My hands flew to my lips. His fingers stilled and slowly rose to the mask covering his face. Slowly he tipped the mask back and smiled apologetically at me. With a small shrug, he let the mask fall back into place. He raised his arms, flicking his fingers in a beckoning motion, reassuring me from the sidelines as ever he had.

Confidence surged inside my chest, swirling there with trust and a heady rush of love.

Zane wouldn't let me fall.

Literally or figuratively.

The music changed tempo, and without missing a beat, Zane took his cue, moving fluidly from behind the curtains, executing the movements as if he'd done them a thousand times. A quick succession of five taps from the flower fairies, and I was off.

There is a <u>Vulnerability</u> displayed in Cady here that is bolstered by the trust she has in Zane. It is <u>Attraction</u> and <u>Emotion</u> rolled into her <u>Reaction</u>.

I moved like a wraith, grace evident in every line of my body, confident in every movement. In, out, over, twist, leg up, arms sweep, twist again and turn. Momentum bunched in the muscles of my thighs, and I sprang for the final leap.

Gasps sounded through the audience as I sailed through the air.

Zane's arms were extended, feet planted, ready for me like he'd been waiting all his life just for this moment.

He caught me exactly as I needed, his palms bracing me against my hips, fingers curling around me securely. My arms spread; legs extended into the air as he turned me. Emotion swelled in my chest as he slowly lowered me with a flourish.

His palm was rough against mine, fingers light against my wrist as he twirled me once, then brought me to rest in front of him.

With trembling digits, I grasped the mask. His hands closed distractingly over my hips as I tugged the mask off, representing the Nutcracker's final transformation. Butterflies swarmed through my middle as I readied myself for the stage kiss of a lifetime.

Green eyes met mine and the world fell away.

"I told you I wouldn't let you fall," he whispered, breath warm on my face.

"Never," I whispered back.

"I think we're supposed to pretend to kiss now," he said with the barest hint of emotion shining in his eyes.

I didn't want to pretend.

Letting my fingers slide along his jaw, I smiled as his eyes widened. Twisting my hand lightly into his hair, I abandoned all caution and planted my lips on his.

The audience erupted into cheers behind us, but it all faded as Zane's lips moved under mine, and his hands dragged me fully flush against him.

We broke away slowly as the audience continued to cheer and clap around us.

"We're going to talk later," Zane whispered, dazed smile covering his face as he gripped my fingers and spun me so we faced the crowd. The rest of the cast filtered in behind us and we took a collective bow. "Also, I still hate tights," Zane said between clenched teeth. I stole a sideways glance at him and noted his flushed cheeks and the tight set of his jaw as he forced his lips into a smile rather than a grimace.

A bubble of laughter worked its way up my throat and burst across my face. I swear, sparklers were shooting out my ears.

I squeezed Zane's hand. "Thank you," I said softly as we bowed again.

"You're welcome. Merry Christmas, Cadence."

"Merry Christmas, Zane."

Strong <u>Attraction</u> paired with <u>Physical Action</u>. There is a moment of hesitation, of intense <u>Attraction</u>, <u>Emotion</u>, and <u>Vulnerability</u> as the different elements combine.

Then The Kiss.

Family and friends met us after, and an impromptu cast party took place backstage. I lost sight of Zane as my parents came and crushed me in a hug.

"You were brilliant!" Mom said, the scent of her rose perfume tickling my nostrils.

"Cadence, I have never been prouder of you than when you flew across that stage!" Dad said as he took his turn, hugging me tight, and placing a bouquet of beautiful Christmas-colored flowers and greenery with little gold sparkles into my hands.

"Cady, I have to tell you something, and I'm afraid it will make you angry. I didn't tell you before because, well, you had enough to worry about."

"Channi, what is it?" I turned worried eyes to my best friend.

"I don't want you to be disappointed, but I don't think I like Jordan. He's nice to look at, but I don't think he's all that nice on the inside. Will you be heartbroken if I decide to like someone else?"

I hugged her. "Never."

"Good. That's a relief. Also, I think Zane is waiting for an opportunity to talk to you. That looked like some kiss you shared. I expect all the details later!" she whispered.

I giggled nervously.

Zane met my gaze across the room and slowly made his way to me. Without a word, he lightly clasped my fingers and led me through the throng of people, silently out into an empty practice room. My heart hammered in my chest as my pulse spiked. The next few minutes were likely going to determine significant things for my life. Nerves and anxiety writhed in my middle as I swallowed.

Once we were alone, Zane faced me, his green eyes intense.

"So. You kissed me." His voice held no trace of discernible emotion.

I swallowed hard again. "I did."

We stared at each other, neither of us sure where to go.

Zane grasps her fingers and Cady feels Emotion, Attraction, and Reacts.

"Do you wish I hadn't? Is this going to alter everything forever?" The words scraped themselves from my throat as dread cramped my belly.

"Oh, it happened. It's definitely going to alter things. Because I want to do it again," he finished softly, slowly stepping into my space. "I don't think you kissed me because that's what the stage directions indicated, Cady."

He was mere inches from me, his green eyes searching mine. My body was practically humming with the electricity crackling between us.

"I kissed you because I wanted to." The words slipped out.

My breath caught as his fingers lightly traced over my waist. "Would it be a problem if I wanted to kiss you back?"

"Only if you didn't."

Zane cracked a smile before his expression sobered as his gaze raked over my face. "Cadence," he whispered.

My hands slid over his forearms, up to his chest. His heart thundered beneath my fingertips as he lowered his head. His lips slowly closed over mine as ecstasy burbled through my veins.

> Here, at last, we have the culmination of the <u>Attraction</u>, the <u>Emotion</u>, the <u>Vulnerability</u>, the <u>Reaction</u>, and the <u>Physical Action</u>.
> ⚘
> The After Kiss is implied as a Happily Ever After.

Now you practice writing a swoony scene between your
characters.

What does each character find attractive about the other?
Think about both emotional and physical characteristics.

What are some vulnerabilities of each character?

Practice writing a swoony scene between your two characters.

Other Romance Thoughts

LUST VS. LOVE

Love and lust are not the same thing.

Love is selfless, putting the needs of others above self. It desires the health of the other despite the wants of the self.

Lust is selfish, putting the needs and wants of self above all else. It is self-indulgent and self-serving. It's possessive. It's greedy. It lacks self-control.

An interesting thing about writing lust versus love is that sometimes the same words can be used to describe both love and lust but with vastly different results. It should be pointed out that in a healthy relationship, there can be an *element* of lust. Of *wanting* the other person. Desire can be a companion of lust, and in a healthy, functioning relationship, desire is a good thing. When attraction and desire are associated with love, these things manifest into goodness. When attraction and desire are associated with lust, when lust is the ruling body, these things are twisted into something malicious. Lust can allow a character to think anything or everything about another character regardless of the other character's thoughts, feelings, or autonomy. When writing, it's important to keep the character's motivation in mind—lust can influence a character to make bad decisions.

Love vs. Lust

Love	Lust
Takes Time	Rushes
Offers Security	Is Jealous
Gives	Takes
Is Patient	Is Impatient
Waits	Is Self Seeking
Unselfish	Violent
Generous	Condemns
Gracious	Self Centered
Extends Mercy	Endangers
Protects	Disloyal
Is Faithful	Abandons

Think about your characters. How would they describe each other? Do those words, thoughts, and feelings seem more like love or lust?

Jot some notes about how they might show love or lust.

____
____
____
____
____
____
____
____
____
____
____
____
____

More Romance Thoughts

WHY SWOON IS BETTER THAN SEX

Sex is pervasive in today's culture. It's everywhere. It's on billboards, on TV, in movies, on cereal boxes and in advertisements. One can hardly even buy a cup of coffee without an advertisement of a scantily clad woman seductively blowing steam onto the would-be patron.

If sex is used to sell cars and cigarettes, of course, sex is used to sell books.

But there is something better than body parts on the page if you want to fulfil your reader's deepest level of satisfaction.

Enter: Restraint.

RESTRAINT

Restraint means holding back, controlling, or holding in check. It implies self-control, discipline, and respect.

It's also one of the most tantalizing things you can include in a book to up the romantic tension.

When characters show restraint toward each other, the tension increases and the romance slows down while the pacing does not suffer. Teasing your readers with little breadcrumbs of romance is a great way to build swoon.

Restraining does not take away from the romance—it *enhances* it.

Once your characters do the deed, the picture is enlarged, and no secrets are left uncovered. The mystery and the attraction dies. There is no more unknown. No more exploration. No more enticement. It's done.

However, when characters show restraint, it's so much more satisfying when they do finally kiss. The moment does not feel cheap or ordinary. It feels special. It feels hard fought and hard won. Restraint adds *value* to the romance. It emphasizes cherishing over physical gratification.

There are lots of good ways to use restraint to heighten the romantic tension. These can range through all of the heat ranges, too. Restraint can be shown in Sweet, Swoony, and Steamy Romance.

Some ways to do this:

Noticing

Awareness

Chemistry (both emotional and/or physical)

Proximity

Attraction

Unfulfilled Desire (characters may or may not recognize their want)

Confession

Vulnerability

Restraint also implies *respect.*

RESPECT

Respect is a sign of esteem, a sense of worth or excellence. How characters interact with each other can be a chief way of communicating their own inner integrity—or lack thereof. Respect is an essential ingredient in a healthy romantic relationship—and it helps build swoon, too. How a character interacts with, where his or her thoughts go, where eyes do or don't go, where hands wander or do not wander, how boundaries are kept or not, are all ways for characters to externally show their inner strength. Respect should not be underrated as a way to establish healthy boundaries between your characters. When one character respects the other, and it shows, that is a way the characters build trust.

When one character shows respectful restraint toward another character, often the reason he or she holds back is to put the needs of others first. Restraint and respect often both comes from a desire to protect, to cherish, to share something deep, meaningful, and valuable with someone. True romance is respectful, giving, and unselfish. It is not immediate gratification. It is not selfish. It is not self-seeking. It is a specific choice to honor the other's values, feelings, or emotions over any selfish wants. It emphasizes cherishing over physical gratification.

And if one is writing a morally gray character, even these dubious leads tend to have a moral code (this is why we root for them!). Restraint shows this deep-seated honor.

Restraint

- Noticing
- Awareness
- Chemistry (both emotional and/or physical)
- Proximity
- Attraction
- Unfulfilled Desire (characters may or may not recognize their want)
- Refusing to touch or kiss
- Vulnerability
- Confession

Restraint and Your Characters

____

____

____

____

____

- Noticing the love interest
- Awareness of the interest's interest
- Chemistry between protagonis[t] and love interest
- Proximity to the love interest
- Unfulfilled Desires?
- Who fell first?
- Does the protagonist find the love

____

____

____

____

____

____

____

____

Even More Romance Thoughts

TENSION

A few notes on tension. The best way to build the swoon through increased tension is to heighten character awareness. Give them restraint—maybe even barely controlled restraint—but also give them impossible chemistry, proximity, undeniable attraction. Make them hot and bothered (to whatever degree your story calls for). Unfulfilled desire keeps your characters searching for that release, and keeps your reader completely immersed and engaged.

This sort of respect, restraint, and tension is also a useful catalyst for shared vulnerability between characters as well. When one character respects the other, and it shows through restraint, then the characters build trust—but more on that later.

Let's pick up with Lainey and Keiran later that spring.

We could still hear the carousel going in the distance. The sun was setting, and everything was bathed in an orange glow. The concrete wall was warm where it had soaked up the afternoon sun, and now the trapped heat sank into my shoulders as I stood close to it. The spring carnival that came every year was still going full force behind the wall by which we now walked on our way back toward campus, but for the moment, we were alone. I tugged Keiran's hand. He glanced at me, and I quirked an eyebrow. He glanced around, a slow grin stretching his lips, and came to a stop beside me. He stared down at me a full minute, sizzling tension building between us, then with tantalizing slowness, his fingers ghosted around my waist and pulled me into him.

My heart pumped, beating erratically as a soft breeze ruffled the hem of my skirt. His hands cupped my hips, drawing me flush against him. I went up on tip toe against him, arms looping around his neck, every part of me wanting his lips on mine. His pulse jumped in his neck as he swallowed. His eyes roved my face, landing on my lips.

I didn't have to wait long. He brought his mouth to mine, covering my lips with his. Together, our heads angled, lips dancing together, sparks flying between us. His hands squeezed my hips, and mine snaked up to tangle in the hair at the base of his neck.

His lips moved and mine responded, more insistent, more wanting, more heat. It felt like forever since it had been just the two of us, just us and this fire that raged between us.

Suddenly, Keiran broke off, his breaths erratic, and leaned his forehead against mine. I blinked, not ready for things to end. We hadn't had nearly enough time for each other with midterms and work schedules, and I missed him. Missed *this*.

"Why did you stop?" I whispered unevenly.

He swallowed hard, pausing before he spoke, voice deep and husky. "I'm afraid."

"Afraid of what?" My fingers played with his dark waves, desire morphing into concern. I knew we hadn't had much time together lately, but now I wondered if maybe I'd missed something—something big—and hadn't seen something Keiran had tried to tell me.

"Afraid that if I kiss you the way I want to, that we'll crash and burn and be over before we even have a chance to give this a real shot. And I want...I want you. So bad." He pulled back and met my gaze. He gulped. I blinked again, heat still building in my middle, as I tried to decipher his words.

Sparkles danced over my shoulders and down my backbone in answer to his impromptu declaration. Desire was a thing inside my chest clawing to get out, to show Keiran that I wanted him back.

"You want me?" I repeated cheekily with a small smile. My finger twirled one of his curls.

He grinned crookedly. "Yeah. But not just, you know, not just in bed." His hands relaxed, sliding up to my waist. "I want this to be...forev—for a really long time. And if we go too fast too soon, we'll kill it."

I stared at him a minute as the wisdom behind his words sank in. When I realized he was holding back in an effort to have *more* with me, my heart exploded.

I love you, I wanted to say. The words pounded along with my pulse, confirming everything Keiran was saying. I wanted Keiran, too. *Forever.*

So help me, I wanted to marry this man.

I wrapped my arms around his shoulders and held him tight. He hugged me close, and we stood there in each other's arms for a long time, unspoken words, thoughts, and feelings flying between us.

There are a lot of high emotions, sparks, and some physical actions that accompany things here. However, note how the pinnacle of these actions works as a catalyst to provide understanding into Keiran's mindset—*why* he stops kissing Lainey. They both want to continue. However, Keiran asserts that what he wants ultimately is not just instant gratification. He wants something longer, deeper, more meaningful with Lainey, and based on his words and actions here, the reader can infer that he feels it is too soon to take their relationship physically beyond where it has already progressed.

This why leads us to Keiran's words and what they ultimately show.

Vulnerability.

VUNERABILITY

Vulnerability is the opening of oneself to another—allowing someone else to see the most tender, potentially painful spots. This vulnerability can allow for the deepest intimacy or the deepest betrayal.

When intimacy is achieved by vulnerability, trust is forged. Any healthy relationship needs to be based on trust and this sort of intimate vulnerability.

This can be a terrifying contemplation. Especially if a character has been wounded in the past. These sorts of wounds can be produced in a variety of ways and from a variety of people—parents, siblings, other romantic relationships, friends, etc. The deeper the relationship, the deeper the betrayal and the wound.

When a romantic interest sees this wound and addresses it with tenderness and the sort of understanding that breeds trust and care, this is another step in the staircase of swoon.

Remember, at the heart of all humans is a desire to be seen and known.

This cannot be fully achieved without vulnerability.

And vulnerability requires exposing one's most sensitive parts—sometimes literally and, frequently, emotionally.

Often vulnerability becomes a defining moment where characters achieve courage and strength and not only reveal themselves to others but also reveal something to themselves.

Real strength and courage are built on truth. And vulnerability, at its heart, is about revealing truth. The truth of past pains. The truth of how a person can be hurt. The truth of what it means to *be*. As these vulnerable truths are revealed to romantic interests, they often reveal things to the characters themselves. They allow the character to grow. To accept, to overcome, to *be*.

In the last example, Lainey realizes both that Keiran desires her more deeply than she had imagined and that he's willing to forego his immediate gratification. He reveals his innermost desires—he becomes vulnerable to her, not only allowing Lainey to see more deeply into Keiran's heart, but also allowing a more abiding sort of trust to bloom inside of her. She understands that Keiran cares for her profoundly, and it is out of respect for her that he takes the actions he does (and his restraint keeps the tension without breaking it).

Vulnerability creates authenticity, builds trust, reveals character depth, and acts as a catalyst to bring them together, or ultimately drive them apart.

Jot down some situations where characters may become vulnerable to others.

Additional Thoughts

Kissing

As we've discussed, there are different levels of kissing.

The type of kiss you establish in your book is completely determined by the context of the story. Things like the characters themselves, the plot, the timeline, the setting, the cultures from which your characters come and the culture they are in at the time of said lip locking, the religious beliefs of the characters, familial pressures, the rules of the society, and the character's personal beliefs.

That's a lot of considerations for something so "simple" as a kiss!

When crafting swoony romance, it's important to remember how your characters react in the face of all these things—because your characters must be the driving force behind the kiss.

Is your hero assertive?

Is your heroine brash?

Is one of them sensitive?

Has one of them faced trauma?

These are all questions to take into consideration. Kissing is not just about the meeting of lips or the brushing of skin. Not every kiss is appropriate for every sort of story. Knowing your genre and the type of romance level appropriate for your story to fit within your genre norms is a must.

As we've discussed, there are also different levels of kissing, and not every kiss is appropriate for every sort of story.

Knowing your genre, and the type of romance level appropriate to your story to fit within your genre norms is a must.

Answer the questions on the following page and think about your own personal comfort level with writing swoon.

MEN AND WOMEN

It is sometimes overlooked that men and women tend to prefer, or desire, different things from a romantic relationship. These differences can come in handy when writing romance.

Women tend to prefer emotional over physical, while men tend to prefer physical over emotional. This is not to say that men or women—either one—are one-dimensional. They're not. But taking into account that women tend to crave emotional connection over physical connection, while most men prefer the opposite, is a good way to build your characters and the tension between them.

Do not forsake all emotion for the physical or vice versa. It is important to remember that both men and women crave connection, regardless of how it is pursued. But some characters may be skewed more one direction than the other. Depending on your character(s) and their backstory, what they find attractive and how they pursue it will vary from character to character.

Part of the fun of a romance is seeing the pursuit. Usually, it is the man who pursues, but not always. Regardless, in a pursuit, there is a *prize* at the end. The building of the swoon is the racecourse the pursuit takes, and that release at the climax, with the final culmination of the tension, is the prize.

Flip the page and peruse a few common emotional and physical preferences that can up the ante in your swoon.

TROPES

Tropes are commonly used themes or ideas, and they are particularly prevalent in romance books.

These can be useful as they are largely universally recognized, and while some can be overdone, many people still enjoy a fresh take on a trope as old as time itself. Some of the most common tropes are:

Friends to Lovers: Where two characters who have known each other for a long time fall in love by the end of the book.

Love at First Sight: A character—sometimes both—falls in love immediately (or at least falls into fascination or interest) as soon as he or she sees the other.

Fated Mates: Similar to Love at First Sight, this trope is often used in paranormal romance or fantasies in which two characters discover they are destined to be together.

Enemies to Lovers: When two characters begin a story as enemies but overcome their enmity or differences by the end of the story and fall in love.

Fake Dating: Two characters typically form an agreement to appear like they are dating each other, and then things get real and they discover that perhaps they want to date each other for real.

Brother's Best Friend/Sister's Best Friend: A character falls for their sibling's best friend. This trope usually contains elements of "off limits" and awkwardness.

Forbidden Love: Circumstances are such that it is not convenient or proper for two characters to fall in love. But they do anyway.

Soul Mates: Much like Fated Mates, two characters are fated to fall in love, or fated to be together, against all odds, sometimes through multiple lifetimes. Used more commonly in non-paranormal, but often fantastical books.

Arranged Marriage: Two characters enter into an arranged marriage often set up by parties other than themselves, but they find themselves falling in love anyway.

Marriage of Desperation/Convenience: When two characters team up/marry to overcome circumstances and find themselves in love by the end.

Hidden Baby: This trope often happens with one-night-stands or relationships that sour suddenly. The woman finds herself pregnant but hides the pregnancy and the baby. However long later, the man finds out, and the pair comes together and makes a family unit. Sometimes a twist can be done on this where the man who becomes the father of the hidden baby is not the biological father but becomes the father figure by choice.

Second Chance: Where two characters were once in a relationship but broke up for a period of time (usually years), and when circumstances bring them back together, they fall in love all over again.

Girl/Boy Next Door: When neighbors who have (often) known each other a long time become close and fall in love.

Unrequited Love: One character pines after another for a significant period of time. This trope can end bitter-sweetly.

Insta Love: Similar to Love at First Sight, this is an instant connection that bonds two characters together. It is more common in paranormal or YA books.

One Bed Trope: A situation in which two characters, who are already attracted to each other, find themselves at a place of lodging where there is only one bed, and they inevitably end up sharing it (usually without sex).

Kissing Factors to Consider

- Characters
- Plot
- Timeline
- Historical Context
- Culture
- Setting
- Religion
- Religious Beliefs
- Society
- Familial Pressures
- Personal Beliefs
- Extenuating Circumstances
- Awareness

FINAL THOUGHTS

I hope this guide has been helpful to you in learning how to craft your own believable swoon. The sections in this guide are set up such that you should be able to revisit them for different types of writing and different levels of swoon.

In the rest of the book, you'll find some additional writing practices and exercises you can do for fun, or for practice.

Go forth! Write all the toe-curling swoon!

Practice Prompts

She's on the debate team, straight laced, and has a hidden love of SciFi. He works for the school's radio broadcast channel and plays basketball for a community team. They find themselves at a party and through no actions of their own, they're shoved into a closet together to play Seven Minutes in Heaven.

It's awkward. Especially since they've been crushing on each other all year.

Practice Prompts

They went on a group hike but got separated from the group when a torrential rain storm hit right at twilight. They found an abandoned cabin in the dark. There's one bed. And one blanket.

The tension inside is crackling like the lightning outside.

Practice Prompts

She is trapped in a marriage of convenience and sees no future, even though she has grown to admire her husband.

Then she overhears him vehemently defending her honor at a dinner party.

The carriage ride home is fraught with delicious tension.

Practice Prompts

They've been practicing for months with their band mates to compete at a national competition. Long nights, long practices, so much effort.

The big night arrives. In the excitement of their epic win, they kiss.

Now they don't know whether to kiss again or pretend it never happened.

Practice Prompts

These office enemies, competing for the same promotion, are forced to share a desk during renovations and their escalating passive aggressive sticky note war comes to a head when they both need the desk at the same time.

Their hands brush, their gazes collide.

Maybe they don't hate each other as much as they thought...

Practice Prompts

The princess has fallen for the young master of the sword. She's engaged to the prince of a neighboring kingdom.

But when the kingdom is invaded, and the sword master saves her, they must go on the run.

He may be able to keep her body safe...but what of her heart?

Practice Prompts

They were childhood friends. He had to move away to go work on a space station, but now he's back in town. They have decided to meet up. They've never quite forgotten each other.

But she just discovered there may be alien DNA in her blood. Is there any hope of romance between them?

Swoony
Language

Swoony Language

- Love
- Like
- Interest
- Awareness

What about romance makes you uncomfortable?

____
____
____
____

Why does it make you uncomfortable?

____
____
____
____

What is the hardest part of writing romance?

____
____
____
____

Do you like writing kissing?

How much description are you comfortable writing in terms of romance?

Does physical affection in books make you uncomfortable?

Is the level of swoon in your book appropriate for the genre and audience?

What do you feel needs the most practice for writing believable swoon?

Swoony Language

Hands

Stroke
Caress
Grasp
Clutch
Crush
Grope
Brush
Feather
Cradle
Grip
Brace

A Chin tip
Thumb over the lip
Slide into the hair
Grip hips
Clutch clothing

Write other swoony words to use for hands.

Swoony Language

Shoulders

Muscular
Broad
Taut
Tension
Rigid
Flex
Stiffen
Bow
Arc
Shiver

Slide up shoulders
Grip the top of shoulders
Feel the flex of muscles
Glide up ribs to shoulders

Write other swoony words to use
for shoulders.

Swoony Language

Eyes

Flash
Snap
Sparkle
Glint
Assess
Rove
Trail
Train
Follow
Gleam
Know
Vulnerability

Hooded
Darken
Dilate
Agonize

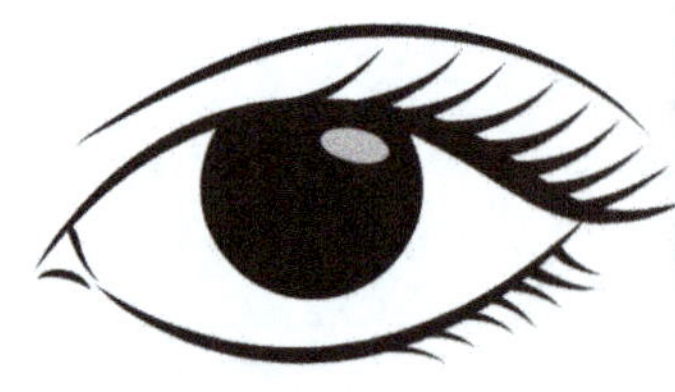

Write other swoony words to use for eyes.

Swoony Language

Lips

Deepened
Pressure
Pucker
Bite
Move
Open
Part
Crack
Suck
Purse

Motionless
Moisten
Lick
Taste

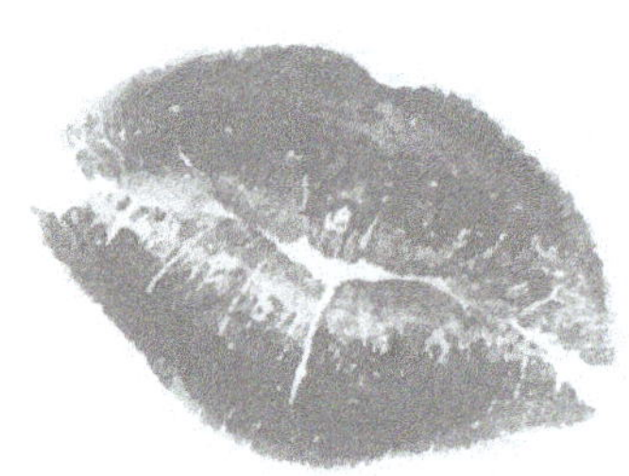

Write other swoony words to use for lips.

Swoony Language

Neck

Curve of the neck
Base of the throat
Vein
Pulsing Vein
Lean back, exposing the neck
Pillar of throat
Column of throat

Write other swoony words to use
for neck.

Swoony Language

Lungs/Breath

Gasp
Suck in a breath
Panting
Stutter
Whoosh
Forced exhale
Breathy
Shallow
Tight

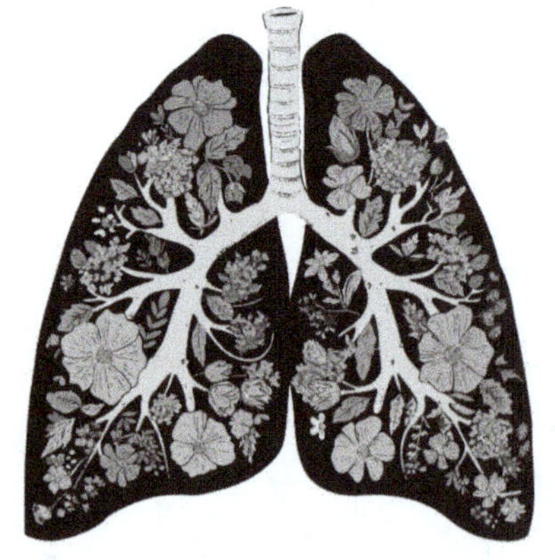

Write other swoony words to use
for lungs/breath.

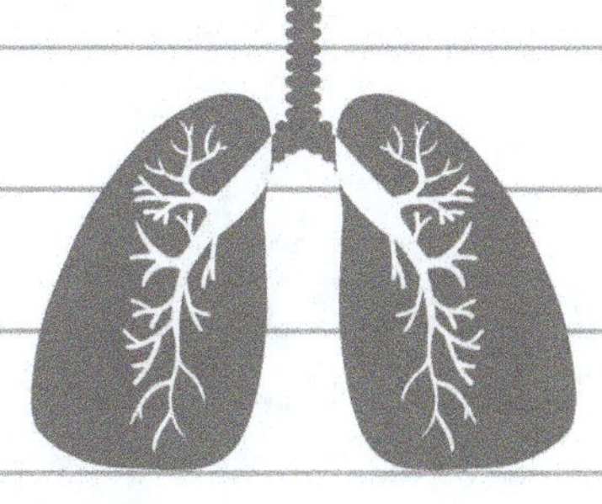

Swoony Language

<u>Skin</u>

Tingle
Flush
React
Goosebumps
Glisten
Damp
Prickle
Awareness

Write other swoony words to use for skin.

Swoony Language

Teeth

Nibble
Bite
Graze
Click

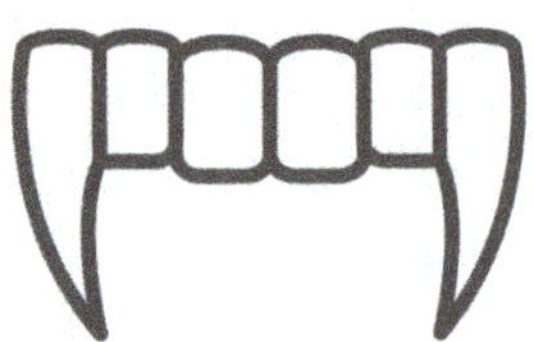

If you're writing fantasy,
there may be other uses for teeth.

Write other swoony words to use for teeth.

Emotional Attractiveness

Available

Integrity

Commitment

Attentiveness

Pursuit

Intellect

Honesty

Kindness

Care

Provider

Protector

Exclusivity

Add Some Others

____

____

____

____

____

Add Some Others

____

____

____

____

____

Physical Attractiveness

Shoulders

Biceps

Thighs

Eyes

Lashes

Voice

Height

Forearms

Veins in arms or hands

Hair

Smile

Scent

About the Author

 Writing books full of murder, mayhem, sometimes magic, and always kissing, **AJ Skelly** (also writing as **April J. Skelly**) is an author, reader, and lover of all things fantasy, medieval, and fairy-tale-romance. And werewolves. She has a serious soft spot for them. As an avid life-long reader and a former high school English teacher, she's always been fascinated with the written word. She lives with her husband, children, and many imaginary friends who often find their way into her stories. They all drink copious amounts of tea together and stay up reading far later than they should.

You can read more about her stories, shenanigans, random factoids, and new books at www.ajskelly.com.

<u>Other Books by AJ Skelly</u>

The Wolves of Rock Falls Series
First Shift
Rogue Shift
Sworn Shift
Pack Shift
Lost Shift

Of Flame & Frost

Murder at Mistlethwaite Manor

An Alliance of Ash and Jade

The Rat King

Kiss and Tell

A Murder Once Forgotten

<u>As April J. Skelly</u>

A Lethal Engagement

Find The Rat King and An Alliance of Ash and Jade on the Lumiview!

Where great stories find new life

LumiView is a new premium vertical storytelling platform bringing immersive story worlds to life — from fantasy and adventure to family and faith-inspired journeys.

Cinematic short-form stories designed for mobile viewing

Emotionally rich worlds across fantasy, mystery, family, and more

Early access to a new generation of uplifting, high-quality storytelling

reated by Y+X Entertainment
xentertainmentgroup.com

Scan to join the LumiView early access community

e the first to discover new stories, worlds, and releases.